INDEPENDENCE DAY$

The Ultimate Win Win Win Strategy
for Financial Security Forever

BLAKE T. TODD

ISBN: 1-4392-1907-9

ISBN-13: 9781439219072

Library of Congress Control Number: 2008910609

Visit www.booksurge.com to order additional copies.

ACKNOWLEDGEMENTS

The acknowledgements that need to be made are almost too numerous to count. During a quarter century in the investment business I have encountered many people who have added to the base of knowledge that makes up this book. There were the people who gave me a chance in the business, those who provided better opportunity, and so many more. But before I can acknowledge them, I must give credit where the most credit is due. I give thanks and acknowledgement to my parents. Roger and Mary raised me, molded me, provided the care and concern, instilled the core values, gave me an education second to none. They provided me with both the school learning and the world wide exposure to ideas, sights and sounds that proved equally as enlightening as any book ever written. They sacrificed much in the pursuit of my sister's and my upbringing, and it is nice to publicly give them the credit they deserve.

The professional acknowledgements are so numerous that I list them here without further ado and without a lot of explanation. Stuart Russell, thank you for the introduction to Bruce Pretzinger whose manager, Tony Garrett, gave me my start in the financial industry at Dean Witter.

At Dean Witter I have a number of people to thank: Chuck Waterman who showed me that short term cash is an investment that makes a difference to the return in an account; George Cassett who demonstrated the value of long term investing; Jim Lee who taught me the concept of working smartly and effectively; Frank Hobbs who was the first and one of the few whom I ever saw retire from the business; Ann Height who demonstrated the value in looking at the economics of partnerships and that you can say no to the firm's offerings. In fact, the whole office was an exceptional mentoring group for a young person in the investment industry.

Barcley Perry, I wish to express my gratitude to you for the opportunity to join Kidder Peabody and to expose me to the myriad of avenues the financial industry has. I also want to include Paul Arentsen, who introduced me to the SRC chart books and my first appreciation for long term trends; Sam Coleman who drove home the value of being a member of various community groups; and Harry Eversole, my first investment partner in managing portfolios . But most important at Kidder Peabody was Richard Kimball, the head of research at Kidder Peabody, who had the most profound affect on my understanding of building portfolios and selecting stocks.

Nine years at the Glendale office of Smith Barney transformed me from being a stock broker to becoming a money manager. Thank you, David Banta, for teaching me the difference between the two. Larry Ruderman imparted the benefits of charting securities for short term benefit. Jimmy Zeutzeous lived the constant discipline of safety of capital and asset allocation. And then there were two of the very best managers in the industry who spent some time in this office. Bill Lee demonstrated that you can entertain all ideas and bring them together with caring to create a productive work environment. Bob Altemus showed the core of the business was about the people in it and that speaking your mind and staying true to your beliefs gives a person the integrity that eventually allows the cream to rise to the top.

Managing a portfolio is not the same as managing a business. John Eislie and Rocky Mills not only accommodated my relocation, but provided me with the opportunity to manage a retail branch within Sutro & Co. I had the distinct privilege to manage the Fresno branch of Sutro & Co. through its transition to RBC Dain Rauscher. During less than hospitable years in the brokerage industry from 1999 through 2004, that office doubled in size. Brokers such as Jim Hutton, Bob Honiball, George Bedrosian, Noel Daniels, Tom Weil and Stan Cooper led the office in every way. Together we took that office to a ranking in the top ten in the RBC Dain Rauscher system, and it was acknowledged as such. We received "Most Outstanding Branch" in both 2003 and 2004.

Many thanks to Roland Seidler whose own spirit of following his passions and doing what is right led him to creating one of the finest regional firms in the country. He recognized my passion for asset management and made my transition to true portfolio management possible. It was a sad day when Roland Seidler passed away. He will always be missed. Thanks go then to Andrew Crowell who is the remarkable managing partner of probably the best regional firm in America today,

Crowell Weedon. He has shown the same can do spirit and entrepreneurship as Roland Seidler and allowed me to work with my private clients at Crowell Weedon as well as manage a mutual fund for the Santa Barbara Group of Funds.

While I am currently employed as a partner of Crowell Weedon & Co., and as a portfolio manager for the Santa Barbara Group of Mutual Funds, the forgoing brief acknowledgements of some of the key individuals along my journey in the investment industry should show that the ideas in this book are a compilation of my experiences through the years as well as the assimilation of knowledge that I have accumulated and molded into my own philosophy. My thanks go to so many who have had a piece in painting the picture of my experiences. There are so many names I did not mention, but they know who they are.

Finally another acknowledgement needs to go out. Call it saving the best for last. Family is special and without them the motivation to do so much of what we accomplish would not be there. Joyce, you are my only sister and bring the counterbalance to my evenness. Together we can get through anything. And thank you, Joyce, for bringing Reid into our family; a better brother no one could ever have. Vanessa and Mason have given without even knowing. Their sacrifice may have been the greatest. They have given up precious time we could have spent together, giving me the hours I have spent pursuing the quest to provide and support them so they can have every opportunity they desire. And still each year I look at our Christmas letter and realize it has been a full and, yes, a hectic life. And of course, once again, thank you, Mom and Dad. Let's face it, without you none of this is possible!

Thanks to all.

WHAT IS FINANCIAL INDEPENDENCE?

You have not just bought a book; you have bought a personal business plan. Another way to look at it is that you now hold in your hands a template, or an equation, for your future. What's more, this is the most important template you can have because it concerns the most basic need you will have for the rest of your life. That need is money to live on, or in the case of this book, money is more accurately defined as "cash flow."

I want you to learn to achieve what I call "financial independence." You have achieved complete financial independence when you have assets that are generating cash flow that is equal to or greater than your needs. This means you are never in danger of spending your assets; you are only spending your cash flow to live your lifestyle no matter what your level of expenses. Having cash flow that comes from secure predictable sources creates emotional financial independence.

Exactly what does financial independence feel like? I would describe it as peace of mind, the kind of peace of mind that lets you sleep without financial worry each and every night. If you want something more literal, take a look at the work of a

Russian philosopher named Maslov who constructed a chart of life's stages based on a triangle. The goal for everyone in the triangle is to work his way to the top.

Of course, the greatest number of people exists in the bottom section of the triangle which represents simple survival. The next step up is comfort. Above that comes a sense of community. And the pinnacle is self-actualization. Most people spend their entire lives in survival mode, and if they do manage to rise to the comfort level, they usually stop. There they often expend all their resources until they are forced to go back to survival mode again. This cycle tends to repeat itself so that the majority of the world's population is stuck at the bottom of the triangle their entire lives.

I choose to work as a financial advisor because I want to help my clients rise to a point where they can forever leave behind concerns about basic survival. I want them to stop worrying about their checkbooks and the financial implications of every decision they make. They can finally stop doing things for survival and comfort. Then they can, if they choose, concentrate on building a sense of community by helping their fellow man.

With financial independence they can finally experience the joy of doing things because they are the right thing to do. This brings a sense of freedom which is too great to calculate. My clients who achieve this often elect to spend more time with their family, explore other parts of the world, or they may find a new sense of community. In fact they often then find a sense of inner peace by volunteering in some capacity to help their own community. They wind up living happier and more fulfilled lives knowing they have become the best they can be.

In other words, financial independence allows my clients to achieve their own personal level of sustainable comfort so they can pursue their greatest purpose in life, however they define it.

My role as an author is to give you the tools to discover a template for yourself, one that will give you the greatest possible peace of mind. Put simply, common sense investing is what I do. Common sense implies that you as readers implicitly know what you should be doing; even if you aren't doing it. But I think it is a bit more complicated than that.

First of all you need to understand one thing about me and what I believe. This is not a get rich quick book. When it comes to the tale of the tortoise and the hare, I am definitely the tortoise. I am looking to help clients and readers get rich safely and as slowly as necessary.

The financial hare is someone who is always looking for the next big thing or is looking for the one perfect money-making move. He is also willing to take on a high degree of risk with much of his money in order to achieve a high rate of return over a short period of time. This usually means he is buying in on the bubble. The problem with this strategy is that by the time the public gets in on a bubble, they are usually the ones left holding the bag. Trying to time the markets and short tern trading almost always loses in the long run.

As a financial tortoise I believe in slowly building your assets over time by a series of moves based on concrete disciplines. You can accomplish this by first controlling your spending. Instead of spending all you earn, I suggest that you should use a portion of your money to buy investments through dollar cost averaging to achieve a diversified portfolio based on proper asset allocation. If you follow my guidelines, your portfolio will also be enhanced by constant compounding and rebalancing.

Why do I use this comprehensive investment model rather than promising you the moon by simply giving you a method to pick great stocks which are bound to appreciate? It's simple. The market always moves in cycles, and what goes up surely will come down, of course, followed by yet another up cycle!

Statistics show that if you were to look at the rate of return of the S&P over the last thirty years, and if you were to look at the appreciation of stocks versus the compounding of dividends, you would see that the compounding of dividends accounted for about forty-two percent of the rate of return. This means that you, as an investor, should use your ongoing cash flow to add additional shares of stock to take advantage of compounding. It is foolhardy to depend on appreciation alone to grow the equity portion of your portfolio. Most of the increased value of your stocks will accrue from constantly adding additional shares through reinvestment of dividends. So as perverse as it sounds, while you are accumulating the shares you actually want the price to go down so you can accumulate more shares. It is only when you are looking to sell that you want the price to increase. There are automatic ways you can do this that will be described in a later chapter. Does this mean I want you to purchase new dividend-yielding shares blindly? Of course not. I have several disciplines for buying stocks, but we'll get to that later as well.

Notice that the goals and statistics I have set out in this book span a thirty year time frame. Most people realize by now that they should have a long term objective as opposed to the 'short term gain' mentality disseminated by the financial media. Unfortunately, to many people, the idea of a long term strategy means only five to maybe ten years. Why? Because that is so often the definition of long term as promulgated by the mainstream media.

Your definition should be very different. Keep in mind that the media have their own point of view which is driven by their need to sell their product. That greater the number of consumers of any particular form of media, (copies of newspapers in circulation, or viewers of television shows, or listeners of radio as examples) the more they can charge for advertising. It is how they get paid. Media take many different forms. They can be as varied as newspapers, magazines, or newscasts, but the one thing they have in common is that their product has to be different every time it comes out in order for people to become repeat consumers of it. This ultimately causes their ad rates to go up.

So no matter what form of media we watch or read, repeat consumers are what determine the advertising rates broadcasters, magazines and newspapers can charge. Therefore, almost all financial media operate in a microscopic time frame which drives them to sensationalize and distort financial events and information. When people focus on media reports, they are not working on a long enough time frame for any sensible investment plan.

When clients ask me how long their investment time frame should be, I tell them it should be as long as they will live (or longer). If a client who is sixty years old consults me for the first time, he is probably assuming we will only be working to build enough assets for him to retire at sixty-five. But I know five years is not nearly a long enough time frame to accrue the necessary financial assets. He and his spouse have a good chance of living at least another thirty years. At the very least they should continue to grow their portfolio to keep pace with inflation. This means they should not only be disregarding the financial news of the day, they should be thinking instead of multiple economic cycles stretching many years into the future. In addition, many people are investing for the legacy they wish to leave to their children and their children's children. That requires careful planning so their investments can be passed down to succeeding generations who have even longer time frames.

We know for certain that there will always be economic or market cycles. When we go into a recession, or even a depression, events have always happened which bring about the recovery phase of the economic cycle. Whenever you invest, you need to understand that you are investing through cycles. Fortunately, this is not a bad thing because the good news is that cycles bring opportunity.

You have probably heard the expression that all investors are driven by two emotions, which are fear and greed. I believe that in reality there is only one emotion at work, and that is fear because it is so much more powerful than greed. Fear is what the financial media exploit.   And isn't greed just the fear of not making as much as the next person?

All too often people make poor investment decisions based on the headline of the day. This means they all too often ignore economic cycles and buy at the top and sell at the bottom because they are not true long term investors.

I believe the most dangerous phrase on Wall Street is, "This time is different." Because of human nature, when the economy is at a bad point in an economic cycle, investors tend to become especially fearful and make mistakes. I think there is no greater proof of the viability of thinking long term no matter how bad the news than The Great Depression. Take a look back at that time period and you will see that if you had invested near the top of the market before the crash, and if you could have waited for the market cycle to end, in your investing lifetime you would have made back your capital and much more.   And, if you had used my investment disciplines back then, had the cash flow to both live and reinvest at incredibly low prices along the way, you would have done even better.

The key to surviving The Great Depression was to do what I propose in this book, secure your cash flow so you don't have to worry about selling off your assets at depleted prices. You could have lived very well during the worst economic period in

America's history if you had done exactly that. What's more, you could have bought additional assets at dirt cheap prices during the low point of America's economic slump and lived even better in the years following the Depression.

The meltdown of the markets as recently as fall of 2008 has once again tested the mettle of most investors. The saying that "this time is different" finally seemed to be true. But if you had constructed your portfolio according to the template I advocate in this book, riding out the uncertainty would be relatively easy for at least seven years.

So, as long as you have a secure cash flow, I say bring on the recessions because they are a time to accumulate assets. As you have no doubt guessed, accumulating assets is not as simple as buying everything that appears to be underpriced. There are disciplined ways to go about picking and choosing which assets you purchase.

This is where understanding my asset allocation model and the discipline of diversification within asset classes is so important. Even if I can't promise to make you rich beyond your wildest dreams, I will do my best to give you peace of mind so that you will be able to ride out whatever storm our volatile economy throws at you.

UNDERSTANDING ASSET ALLOCATION AND MY MODEL PORTFOLIO, DIVERSIFICATION, AND REBALANCING

Even during The Great Depression the economy did not go down the drain all at once. During that catastrophic time it tended to go through different phases as different industries went bad. We can use the lessons learned from The Great Depression as a guide to investing today even though our model is one of extremes which we hope never to revisit.

Fortunately, in a depression (or far more likely, in a recession) the first industry that goes down will shake itself out and those that remain will tend to recover the most dramatically in the next recovery. Those surviving companies will be stronger, have a greater market share and lead the recovery. This does take some time, and the prices of the securities have to go through a process called bottoming out. That bottoming out phase is usually the most opportune time for investors to take note and begin investing in the depressed industry. Unfortunately the vast majority of the public is not focused on that. Instead they are focusing on CNBC, or *The Wall Street Journal,* recounting whatever is the worst new financial disaster of the day. Fear is one of the most powerful tools there is, and the media like to play upon investor fears. My mother has recounted to me more than once the remembrances of her parents' agony in the great depression. They lost everything, and her father was out of work for several years. The fear has never left her or others from her generation and those in the media know it and play upon those fears. If the financial press media were truly doing their job to help investors, they would instead focus on those industries that have already bottomed out and are now showing signs of recovery.

In order to ensure safety, you need to be truly diversified. This means that during a bad economic cycle you might well have a portion of your portfolio that is down substantially. It is probably making headlines in the news and is part of the industry cycle that is being hit hard. You might even be experiencing a troublesome decline in more than one portion of your portfolio depending on how broadly diversified you think you are. Sector rotation is crucial to riding out the rough patches in our economy.

When most people think of such sector rotation, they are thinking only of stocks and which sectors of the stock market or which industries under or over perform at different points in the economic cycle. But it is my purpose to show you that there is a more important type of sector rotation. That is sector rotation among asset classes.

These asset classes go in and out of favor as well. The asset classes that are crucial to a balanced portfolio consist of stocks, bonds (or fixed income) and commercial real estate. Most investors are familiar with the theory that when the stock market is out of favor, it is probable that the bond market will be performing well. I believe that a third asset class is essential to balance volatility in a portfolio, real estate.

To be sure there are some minor asset classes, including precious metals and collectibles. But when it comes to investing your money wisely, you should be looking at only the three asset classes named above because they are the ones that provide the *cash flow* for you to live on. It might surprise you to learn that bonds comprise the largest asset class in terms of total invested capital. Real estate comes in second, and, in spite of all the attention paid to them, stocks are last.

In order to demonstrate the effect of diversifying your money among asset classes, I am going to assume all three asset classes are equal thirds of what I call your "model portfolio", and they go through different cycles at different times. This is what is known as negative correlation. This happens because each asset class has different influences impacting it at different times in the economic cycle.

Fortunately, negative correlation can smooth out the volatility in a portfolio. Often investors lose all perspective and think every asset class is down during certain periods because they are, as usual, listening only to news pundits. And for some reason, the most vociferous news pundits tend to be bears who want to raise their profile by instilling fear into the hearts of investors. But consider the early summer of 2008 when everything looked so bleak there appeared to be nowhere to hide. Government Bonds were actually up! They just weren't given any attention by the media who consider a discussion of bonds a real ratings killer.

The problem does not just lie with the media. Almost every investor has a bias for or against certain asset classes. I have yet to meet a new client who did not come to me with their own preconceived investment equation. One of the most difficult challenges I face is helping my clients overcome their personal preferences in order to do what is prudent. And what is always prudent is to be fully diversified among asset classes and sectors within those asset classes. The negative correlation that results is what brings the opportunity to build additional wealth over the long term if you incorporate the discipline of buying low and selling high.

When I speak of diversification within each asset class, I am speaking of holding different types of investments that don't duplicate each other. For example, if you hold a variety of mutual funds which make up your equities allocation, they need to be different types of funds. You might distribute your mutual funds among value, growth, blue chip, global, and possibly emerging markets. I suggest you go to Morningstar.com to look at the ratings of the funds you are considering and also to look at their major holdings. You don't want two funds that mirror each other in the stocks they own, because you will lose diversification. And if you decide to own equities individually as well, they should be different from the major holdings in your mutual funds.

Surprisingly, there is such a thing as too much diversification within the equities portion of your portfolio. Here is how this can happen: If you own one stock, and it goes down to zero, you have lost one hundred percent of your portfolio. If you own two stocks, and one goes down to zero, you have lost fifty percent. With three stocks the proportion becomes thirty-three percent. By the time you get to your tenth position, you have lost only ten percent. With eleven stocks, you have lost only about nine percent. As you can see, the difference between the tenth and eleventh position and the amount of loss you suffer by diversifying further is now a very small amount incrementally. I believe you are minimally diversified when you have ten positions. This, therefore, is the lowest prudent number of stocks for an individual investor to hold. Many individual investors will stop at ten positions because it is quite difficult to keep up with the homework required for more stocks than that. Most analysts at major Wall Street firms will only follow up to 25 companies, and they do it for a living! However, there is some value to adding more stocks to a portfolio. Just as there is a point of diversifying statistically the risk out of a portfolio, there is a point at which a person can be overly diversified, and the added return from any one position would no longer be meaningful to a portfolio. In my opinion that is at 30 positions. So the optimum portfolio will have between 10 and 30 positions in each asset class.

If you are diversifying within fixed income, you might want to have a portion in high-paying money market funds, CDs with different maturities, a variety of government and corporate bonds, and even some preferred securities. In addition to diversification, for those who are extremely risk adverse, you also can insure your investments against loss by sticking to institutions which protect deposits through insurance by the FDIC or have some other form of government guarantee. Finally, if you want to diversify your holdings in commercial real estate, you can do so by buying Real Estate Investment Trusts (REITs) in a variety of sectors such as office buildings, apartments, retail, or warehouses to name a few. Or you can buy mutual funds comprised of REITs. You can also buy commercial real estate directly by following the guidelines I present later in this book.

Often my clients are frightened by certain types of investments because they are afraid of what they perceive as unacceptable volatility. They may feel that I am asking them to exceed their personal level of risk tolerance. However, risk tolerance is not so much a volatility issue as it is a cash flow and liquidity issue.

I must start with the premise that my clients should never be forced to liquidate their principal for basic living expenses. As a direct result of this focus, the values they see on their monthly investment statements which represent their net worth are not the most important measure of day-to-day success. What they should be focusing on instead is the cash flow their investments generate. The cash flows into their accounts should fund the income needs of the client first and then be utilized in rebalancing the account on an ongoing long term basis. But more about rebalancing later.

Admittedly there are times when someone may need to access their principal for unforeseen emergencies or even special investment opportunities. My model portfolio of dividing your assets among the three classes provides more liquidity to do exactly that. My asset allocation model portfolio also has a hedge against almost every form of risk. Usually that hedge is two-thirds of the portfolio.

I do have a story of a client who learned the hard way the lesson of proper asset allocation and diversification:

My client had his entire IRA in one stock for over twenty years. It was a high tech stock, and he really believed in it. He rode it all the way up as it rose in value, and unfortunately he rode it part of the way back down. This was not even a company he worked for; he just liked its products. However, one day he became unsettled as he happened to watch a televised press conference about his favorite and only investment. He, and apparently many others, noticed that the usually charismatic president of the company appeared to be in disturbingly poor health.

After that appearance the company's stock dropped fifteen, then twenty points. After two decades of investing in the high tech giant, this big drop became a cue for him to sell all his shares. He then came to me wondering if he had done the right thing by getting out or should he buy it all back? The important factor was that this investment was all the money he had, which was about a half million dollars. At the time he was sixty-six, and with increasing age his income had gone down. My client was self-employed and simply unable to take on as many jobs as he had in his youth. He did have a small social security stipend, but he badly needed the additional income.

In spite of all the ups and downs, my client was still in love with that single stock so one of my questions to him was, "How much is enough?" Like so many of the tech companies at that time, his was not generating any cash flow to him, the investor, in the form of dividends. So no matter what the stock value was, it would never be enough because he was never going to get to spend it.

Ultimately he began to understand the mistakes he had been making with his investment. First of all I pointed out the dangers of living with substantial market volatility by asking him what he would do if the one stock he owned went down another ten percent. He replied by saying, "I wouldn't be able to sleep at night." I also asked him if this is what his investments should do because this one company seemed to be taking years off his life. Didn't he want to be in something that would allow him to enjoy life instead of going to the Internet daily to check on the value of his company? Would he not be happier working only for the clients he liked and not worrying constantly that he would be kicked out of his rented apartment due to insufficient cash flow?

We went through the risks of non-diversification and looked at how volatility can be controlled not only by asset classes but by assets within each class. I also showed him an income and growth portfolio, and he said in surprise, "This is more than I am making now." In other words he could do better living off the assets he had accumulated rather than by working.

A light went on in his mind, and he realized that enough is enough. In other words, he was at a stage in which the income from his asset pool could be sufficient to sustain his lifestyle. Even better, with proper allocation his asset pool could still grow year after year. That took a tremendous burden off my client because even if his assets went up and down in total value, the cash flow he needed would still be there. What's more, the very nature of asset allocation and diversification would protect him. He saw that even if his stocks were to go down, chances are his bonds would go up.

The goal for him and for all my clients is that they live less stressful lives on a day to day basis. You just have to learn to follow the formula.

Again, the concept of having three asset classes that are negatively correlated (which means they do not move in the same direction at the same time) is to take the volatility out of your portfolio's performance. This strategy also allows you to participate in industries that are in asset sectors that you might not be able to participate in otherwise.

For instance, many sixty and seventy year old people are wary of holding stock. That's not surprising. If you look at the performance of stocks over a very short period of time such as one year, you may be too nervous to invest any portion of your portfolio in equities. But if those investors would just take a longer term view, as actuarial tables tell us they should, they would see that stocks have done extremely well over a long period of time. This means that they should always want some exposure to stocks no matter what their age. And again, they may be investing for not just their lifetime, but for their beneficiaries as well.

However, as my clients age, I make sure the relative proportion of their *income producing* securities grows to meet their cash flow needs. But I still want to make sure they do not miss out on the gains in the stock market because they are always going to need that growth as an inflation hedge.

My goal is to keep you and my clients invested in equities for a number of years so the excellent long term rate of return will be so obvious that everyone will keep at least some portion of their portfolio in the stock market. The same thing goes for assets such as bonds and real estate. What you will gain by using my equally weighted model portfolio is a hedging component that also works well over the long term.

Among the greatest problems in delivering a constant cash flow is the ravaging effect of inflation. This is one of the reasons you need to hold a third of your portfolio in commercial real estate. Commercial real estate is one of the truest hedges against inflation because as a market it responds more to the effects of inflation than anything else. There may be a slight lag time as it takes awhile for rents to adjust upward, but again we are long term investors, and the lag time is insignificant over the long term.

Stocks of great companies are also inflation hedges because the amount investors are willing to pay for them will go up in tandem with the value of corporate earnings. The earnings of these firms will inflate over time as inflation increases both the gross revenues and earnings per share. As you can see, two thirds of my model portfolio acts as an inflation hedge, which is a very comfortable amount.

On the other hand, bonds do not inflate in value over time, but your other investments in real estate and stocks should mitigate against that shortcoming. Obviously wherever you have a hedge against inflation, you also have the risk of deflation even though it is a much smaller risk. Bonds are the only hedge we have against a deflationary environment, a problem that has shown itself to be less likely over time. As you can see, what I have constructed is a model portfolio which protects you against the greatest risk probability while maintaining a reliable cash flow through real estate and fixed income investments.

Again, for simplicity's sake I am using an asset allocation mix of one third, one third and one third for each asset class. In order for my model portfolio to work, you must have the discipline to rebalance at least every year. This means that you will be forced to sell at the high end of whichever asset class has moved up the most. For example, if real estate has gone up so much that it now represents forty percent of your portfolio, you would be forced to sell roughly seven percent so it now represents one third of your holdings.

What do you do with that seven percent? You put it into the asset classes that have gone down. Rebalancing forces you to buy low and sell high. Therefore, it is a great mechanism to add incremental value over time.

The remaining question is whether rebalancing only once a year is sufficient. There are a number of studies that look at the effect of more frequent rebalancing, and there does not appear to be much difference if you rebalance every quarter instead of every year. You need to give your portfolio enough time to perform or at least make discernable moves before making rebalancing decisions.

When I tell you to rebalance every year, what I really mean is one year and one day. That way you can take advantage of long term capital gains tax benefits. This method does not mean that you should go by the calendar year and rebalance every January first.

 Some investors are wary of rebalancing at the end of every year because of the effect of big institutional money managers on the markets. The perception is that these managers will be rebalancing their own multi- billion dollar portfolios and causing greater disruptions in the prices of securities. But the effect of year-end selling is surprisingly low. In fact most institutional managers rebalance every quarter.

Certainly some tax loss selling does occur at two different "ends" of the year. The first is the calendar year and the second is October 31st. October 31st has become important as the fiscal year-end for a vast number of mutual funds in America. Both of these year-ends can produce what is known as "the angel effect" on the first five business days following year-end. Fallen Angels are stocks that have been subject to tax loss selling at the end of a year because they were already down in price. But at the end of the year when people are done selling and the New Year starts, those people who have been sellers are usually done with selling. In the absence of selling pressure, buyers often push the price of the stock up in the New Year, back to a level that reflects the true value of the company.

This is going to be the same for all asset classes. So if you are selling one asset class and it happens to be slightly lower because it is the end of the year, the asset class you are buying will be lower also. This means you are buying and selling in the same environment.

What I am trying to impress upon you is the importance of rebalancing on an annual basis without fail. Just pick a date you are sure to remember such as your birthday. The actual date you pick is basically meaningless. What is meaningful is your unwavering consistency and commitment to rebalancing.

In reality when I manage my clients' money, the percentage in each asset class ebbs and flows due to where we are in the cycle of that asset class. In addition to serving individual clients, I also manage a mutual fund, and the investments in that fund are also subject to cycles. In managing that fund I stick to the discipline of never exceeding fifty percent in any single asset class. On the other hand, my minimum is fifteen percent in each of those asset classes. This way I am never totally out of an asset class, and you shouldn't be either.

The last thing you want is to discover that your holdings have slowly morphed into a single asset class portfolio. If I do have fifty percent of my mutual fund in one asset class such as equities, and my fund consists of fifteen percent in fixed income and fifteen percent in real estate, I might be holding the remaining twenty percent in cash. But remember, for me cash is in reality short term fixed income because I always require some kind of return on all my investments. So even my cash is structured to give me some degree of cash flow. This means that actually thirty-five percent of my mutual fund is in fixed income. If I find myself in that position, I make sure that the average duration of that fixed income is very short in order to lower the risk of having that much of my portfolio in this particular asset class.

If I were to look backwards in time and arrive at the optimum asset allocation mix, I would be forty percent in stocks, forty percent in real estate, and twenty percent in fixed income. However, for the average person who is reading this book, my model of dividing your portfolio into thirds will be the easiest to manage and rebalance every year.

As it turns out, if you were to test this model over the last twenty years, your portfolio would have grown within ninety-five percent of the S&P rate of return with only sixty percent of the volatility. This is exactly what you as investors want to accomplish: lowering the risk of the markets while optimizing their rate of return. This gives you a way to get the historical rate of return of every asset class by melding the three together.

As a professional I can probably do better because I can, at the appropriate times, underweight or overweight the three asset classes according to their cycles. What I have just described is the tricky discipline of looking for short term trends and deciding whether or not I can use them to my advantage. This practice is commonly known as market timing. The old adage that you have no doubt heard is certainly true: market timing is something best left only to the most experienced professionals, and even they don't always get it right.

I wish I could show you examples from my clients who have invested with me over the last two decades, but I can't because their portfolios have been customized specifically for them to deliver the appropriate cash flow with the appropriate risk. However, I invite you to look at the results of my publically traded mutual fund as an example of my asset allocation, diversification, and rebalancing theories in action.

EQUITIES

As a fellow financial advisor once said to me, "Investing has become everybody's favorite sport." Of course that was when the market was booming. Nowadays investing has become a lot tougher. But the fact remains, everyone who dabbles in the stock market likes to talk the talk, but very few people truly know how to walk the walk.

Perhaps that's why so many people reading this book have lost money in the stock market. No matter how much financial television you watch and how many magazines and newspapers you read, it all amounts to little more than background noise. No television commentator is going to tell you how to build a portfolio, pick stocks and sell when the time is right.

My job is to teach you a clear and disciplined way to pick stocks and make money from them. This is not a lesson in getting rich quick. If you want to be the investor who discovers the next Microsoft or Dell Computer in hopes of turning a few thousand dollars into a million, this is not the book for you. My system of investing is all about harvesting real cash from equities. It's not about guessing tomorrow's lottery winners on the stock markets.

Prepare yourself to hear an approach to the stock market you have never heard before. The basics of this discipline are very easy to understand. Follow them and you *will* make money from the market. It's as simple as that.

How can I make such a bold claim? By building a methodology that revolves around one simple theme: if a stock isn't putting cash in your pocket it shouldn't be in your portfolio. Unless you are harvesting more and more cash from the market every year, you will never achieve financial independence. It is financial independence, having enough money to live comfortably and happily for the rest of your life, that is your aim.

Hitting the jackpot and becoming the next American billionaire by day-trading are fantasies that have lured many investors to ruin. But financial independence is a goal you can actually achieve, and I intend to show you how.

One problem in dealing with equities is that many investors think they already understand completely how they work. The mainstream media and the Internet are loaded with all kinds of information on equities, but you need to know how to filter it and how to interpret it. You also need to know how to put this glut of information into perspective. If you are not a surgeon, you would not dream of operating on yourself. If you are not a financial analyst, you don't really know how to pick stocks.

You are no doubt exposed to investment advice all the time. Pretty much everyone has heard of *Money* magazine. In their January issue they always give you a list of stocks and funds to buy for the upcoming year. If you look at each of the succeeding eleven issues for the calendar year, you will see among the headlines yet another investment into which to put your money. Most people don't have the funds to buy every stock or mutual fund suggestion that *Money* makes, and even if they did, they would be eaten alive by the transaction costs. Furthermore, each month the magazine's recommendations seem to be completely different.

The worst part is that you never see a sell recommendation on any of the stocks or funds you have been told to buy. After all no member of the media wants to anger its advertisers. There is a lot of advice on buying equities that is both promotional and institutionalized. I would also add that it is often highly sensationalized.

My advice begins here. Turn off the television and forget about the "experts" who talk incessantly about the money to be made from buying the latest big thing. Put away your investment magazines and publications as well. I recall one colleague who referred to them as "financial pornography." Why such harsh words? Because investment magazines are all about promoting financial products and selling advertising. Their job is to get you excited about scoring a fortune on the next big thing. They want unsuspecting readers turning pages and then buying the mutual fund, the index fund or the Exchange Traded Fund (ETF) that is really paying for the publication.

Don't forget that glossy magazines are "put to bed" (as they say in the industry) a month or more before publication. In today's volatile, twenty-four hour financial and news cycles, they will not be able to provide useful investment tips if they are a month or two behind the times.

Stock tips are not what this book is about. In fact avoiding stock tips and focusing instead on a disciplined methodology is the key to success.

One word stands at the heart of this methodology: dividends. As I told you, the fundamentals are simple. Cash is king. Stocks that pay dividends should be putting cash into your pocket or into your portfolio with clockwork regularity. Collect enough cash from wise investments, and you will have found financial independence.

Putting it another way, prudent equity investing is all about *cash flow*. Remember this central rule. It applies to all of the chapters in my book. If an investment isn't putting money in your pockets, it's an expense. If an equity isn't paying you regular dividends, it is a gamble and a potentially costly one.

Many investors go about evaluating a company the wrong way. The first thing they tend to look at is the Price to Earnings Ratio. While this is a useful tool for pricing a company in the marketplace, the P/E ratio does not represent the earnings that a shareholder actually receives as cash flow. The only earnings that an investor can ever be certain of spending are from a company's dividends.

Many stock picking guides recommend choosing equities according to their P/E ratio in hopes of finding a company that is undervalued. But I want to you to begin narrowing down your search by selecting *only* companies that offer dividends. Positive cash flow is an absolute must for companies that qualify for your portfolio, and you will be surprised after we screen prospective companies how few investments do qualify for your portfolio.

Many experienced investors will be familiar with an impressive-looking chart which shows the performance of the stock and bond markets since 1926. Elegantly framed charts like the ones I will describe are displayed prominently in the offices of financial advisors all over the country. The great folks at a company called Ibbotson gathered an immense amount of data to create these charts. If you have not seen one of their charts, I recommend you contact them and obtain one. The chart seems to show that stock prices have risen in a spectacular fashion since the Great Crash of 1929. The graph of the value of money invested in the stock market substantially outperforms that of the bond market, treasury bills, and inflation. It's definitely true that stocks have risen in value substantially over the past eight or nine decades. That's wonderful, but there's a much more important fact buried in the well-known skyrocketing stock graph.

The little-known secret of America's spectacular stock market rise is the role of dividends. In fact, dividends have been a huge part of the return from equities throughout history. Since 1926 the average yield of the S&P 500 has been just under 4%. Many of the companies depicted on this famous chart have disappeared, and many others have risen in value. But dividend paying corporations have always contributed real cash flow to the performance of the stock market over many years. The creator of these charts has proven that almost two thirds of the increase in the stock market returns is from reinvested dividends. This is the amazing power of compounding! Einstein called it the eighth wonder of the world.

I believe that the baby boom generation will demand higher dividends from their investments in the future, and I will be at the head of the line voicing those demands. As shareholders we will demand that corporations pay higher dividends, and if they do not, we will simply choose another investment. My policy is to favor investments in those companies that have a history of paying increasing dividends to their shareholders.

But let's get back to the steps we need to take to build a portfolio with positive cash flow. The Price to Earnings Ratio became popular among investors who wanted a way to put a value on an entire business. The P/E ratio essentially tells a business buyer how high a price he is paying for a company relative to its earnings. But if you're not buying the entire business, you won't be seeing any of those earnings unless there is a regular dividend payout. The company will not be sending you a penny of cash you can use to buy groceries or compound for retirement.

Here's another thing to keep in mind: most corporations retain a portion of their earnings in order to grow the company's operations. The company hopes that its expansion will generate greater revenues, more earnings and ultimately the value of the corporation and its stock will rise. That's what many shareholders are also hoping, but there are no guarantees. Wall Street is littered with stories of companies that have used enormous amounts of money to expand rapidly, only to fall far short of their ambitions leaving shareholders holding the bag. Attempting to reap profits by buying stocks of rapidly expanding companies is always riskier. Without a crystal ball no investor can be certain of a company's future performance.

Make no mistake. I don't have an argument with companies that retain a reasonable portion of their earnings in order to develop a business, modernize it and keep it competitive as the business world changes. But I see all equity investors, ordinary people like you and me, as the real owners of the companies in which we invest. Some earnings should always come our way, and those earnings should come to us in the form of increasing dividends.

Why should they pay dividends? Corporate management is managing *my* money, and they have to make decisions about the money the company earns every year. They can, if they choose, reinvest it in the business. Or they can give it back to me, the shareholder, and let me decide what I personally want to do with the money. When they start giving money back to the shareholders, I know that the management fully understands that they are not the true owners of the business. They realize that the shareholders are the owners of the business who deserve a good solid return on their investment.

Most corporations will eventually adopt a dividend distribution policy as their business matures and their stream of earnings becomes stable and predictable. A regular dividend payout makes their stock much more attractive. By contrast, new and rapidly changing companies will hesitate before offering a dividend for a very good reason. If their cash flow is not stable and reliable, the corporate board might be forced to lower its dividend payout or suspend its dividend entirely in order to keep the business running smoothly.

But that kind of drastic action would send a very negative signal to the stock markets and cause share prices to drop sharply. The markets will always interpret a dividend cut to mean that corporate earnings are drying up and that the company itself may be in danger of failing. All corporate executives are aware of this fact, and therefore few companies will take the risk of starting to distribute dividends if they don't feel very strongly that they can continue to make payments to stockholders reliably. That's why a dividend payout sends such a clear message to investors that corporate managers are confident about future earnings.

This brings us to the second key point when we choose among companies that do make dividend distributions. Most corporations will adopt a dividend distribution policy that is sustainable. In other words once they pay out a dividend at a particular rate, they will want to be able to pay at that rate for the foreseeable future. Companies will not pay out all of their earnings. They need a cushion, ensuring their ability to continue operations and pay regular dividends even when profits undergo temporary declines.

What we are looking for as investors is a company that pays out a very conservative portion of its profits so that it always has a cushion to protect itself against the dire consequences of a dividend cut. As the company's profits increase, the board can decide to increase their dividend. This is exactly what we are looking for to grow the value of our investment and keep pace with inflation.

As investors, we want companies that do *more* than pay a dividend. We are looking for corporations that have paid out their dividend consistently without missing a payment or cutting their dividend yield for a reasonably long period of time. As I said, any dividend cut is a warning sign that corporate management does not have a reliable fiscal policy or revenue stream.

Among companies that have made the cut so far, we need to find a way to pick out the very best to include in our portfolio. Among the many companies that have paid out a regular dividend there are some that have increased their earnings and increased their dividends over time. Companies that have a history of consistently increasing their dividends demonstrate a desirable combination of fiscal health and a sensible record of rewarding stockholders directly for their shared ownership of the firm.

That's the kind of company I want my clients to own. I want stable growth and increasing cash flow to shareholders. There are investors who might prefer a high-flying new stock over a stable, steadily growing firm. My advice is to be very careful about companies that are soaring one day, only to face the danger that they will fall back to earth on the next. Dividends are a sign of stability. Increasing dividends are a sign of real financial strength. While it might be tempting to simply buy the stock that is paying the highest dividend, it can be risky. Later in this book you will find a chapter called "Research Tools for Investing." You will find there the means to compare the metrics of a stock to others in its sector. If you find the dividend payout is far above that of the rest of the sector, I would delve deeper to find out the reason why. The dividend rate must be substantiated by good metrics for the rest of the business.

Keep in mind one important fact; dividends don't come directly from earnings. They are *real cash* distributions. This is an important distinction and I'll explain why.

The reported earnings that are used in the all-too-familiar Price-to-Earnings Ratio may be terribly misleading. The accountants who write earnings reports have a great deal of leeway in deciding what to include. I'm not saying that most corporate accountants are dishonest. Far from it. But the rules of accounting allow corporate number crunchers to include a variety of surprising and sometimes unexpected things on the plus or minus side of the balance sheet.

A perfectly honest balance sheet may include exotic entries for items like depreciation, reserves, reversals of prior reserves, goodwill and many other unfamiliar financial items. There's often a good reason for this. Corporate managers may decide to withhold some earnings in order to keep them in reserve for an upcoming quarter that is expected to be slow. Expenditures might be reported the moment a company makes a capital purchase. Or the company may decide to report the drain on its overall earnings only when actual payments are made.

As the collapse of Enron demonstrated all too vividly, the rules of accounting can be stretched beyond the prudent or creative to the outright criminal. If unscrupulous executives are cooking the books, earnings may sometimes be posted when companies have at best only an expectation of income such as the signing of a contract. In the case of a company like Enron, expected income was registered as actual earnings. Losses were hidden in offshore shell corporations. Not surprisingly, Enron was a fast-rising stock, popular with momentum investors. It was not a dividend payer, and we all know what happened.

That's why I strongly recommend focusing on actual cash reserves and especially *cash flow* in a corporate balance sheet if you want to know about the true financial health of a company. After all, a company's cash flow is where our income as shareholders, our dividends, comes from. If you want to learn how to read a company's balance sheet as well as other financial data, you should go to the chapter entitled "How to Read Financial Statements" and look at Exhibit 1.

Try to think of an earnings report as a blend of all the positives and all the negatives about corporate performance. It is a company's carefully constructed attempt to put its best face forward and, as I described, earnings reports can be misleading. By contrast, cash flow is a very simple, straightforward number and that makes it much harder to manipulate.

Because a company's cash flow is such a transparent indicator, I believe it provides a much truer measure of a firm's financial health than most other metrics on the balance sheet. Increasing cash flow year after year is a convincing sign of a healthy company. That brings me to the next key step in narrowing down our search for companies that merit a position in your portfolio.

I suggest you look for companies that have *increasing cash flow per share* on a consistent basis. This is a much more reliable indicator than the easily-manipulated earnings per share. If earnings per share have been manipulated, the much-discussed P/E ratio will be a misleading indicator. But, if cash flow per share is increasing steadily, it's a good bet that dividends per share can also increase over time.

There's one other measure which I believe is crucial if we want to determine how a company is performing for its shareholders. That measure is called "Return on Shareholder Equity." Very simply, "Return on Shareholder Equity" presents a measure of the profits a company has generated relative to the total investments that shareholders have made in the company. The higher the ratio, the more money a company is generating for every dollar you have invested in it.

My goal is to find corporate management that can consistently employ the capital at its disposal, your shareholder equity, to deliver a superior rate of return on your investment. So, the next step in the process is to screen my investment candidates even further to find companies that consistently deliver much better than average rates of return on equity. Finding a company that delivers superior equity returns year after year counts for a lot more in my books than a company that surprises the market with an unexpectedly stellar share price performance during a single year, or a single quarter.

Finding a company's "Return on Shareholder Equity" is relatively simple using the many user-friendly tools on the Internet. The Internet also provides information on the history of a company's dividend yield. I hope you will take advantage of the chapter later in the book to help you with this process.

Unlike most individual investors, professional financial advisors have sophisticated screening tools to filter the entire universe of stocks in search of our key criteria. Advisors should also have resources that can track our key measures of corporate performance over a twelve-year period. It's important when evaluating a company to look as far back as possible in order to ensure that it has delivered increasing dividends, increasing cash flow and return on equity.

Okay, we have finally screened the world of stock offerings to find positive indicators of corporate health as we make our investment decisions. That still leaves a lot of companies to choose from. What about negative indicators? Are there warning signs we should keep watch for, even if corporate dividends and cash flow satisfy our demands? Not surprisingly, there are several.

First we look for anything that might jeopardize a company's cash flow. The biggest risk would be outstanding demands for the cash that the company generates. If those demands have to be satisfied before the dividends can be paid, then the reliability of the company's all-important dividends might also be at risk.

There are also threats to cash flow in corporate obligations such as debt service and lease expenses.

In short, we do not want companies that face large debt service payments or other financial obligations that could disrupt cash flow. Judging these risks may be a task that is too difficult for novice investors. That's because there is no hard and fast rule dictating that a company can only have a certain percentage of its balance sheet in debt. Some companies, such as utilities, enjoy very predictable, sustainable cash flow and stable revenues. That allows them to hold more debt without risk to the bottom line.

Nevertheless, as a general rule, I prefer companies that have lower levels of debt. Firms that keep control of their debt load have a far better chance of paying out dividends as expected and, hopefully, increasing dividends periodically.

Finally, after much statistical screening, we have excluded thousands of companies that do not meet our standards for increasing dividends, improving cash flow, and acceptable returns on shareholder equity and manageable debt loads. We can now get down to fundamental analysis. We can look at the businesses of our remaining target companies and get to understand them and their investment merits. We must look at a company's position in its industry, the health of that industry, and the catalysts that could affect the company or the industry in which it operates.

I believe this is the area of stock analysis that is as much an art form as it is a science. It requires painstaking research into each company. We have to know how a company earns its revenues and how it competes against its peers. We need to learn about the future prospects of the entire industry in which the company operates. For instance, some businesses that were once considered exotic and highly profitable such as computer manufacturing have become commoditized. That means all competitors in the field make more or less the same product. As a result cutthroat price competition eats away at the bottom line and makes earnings unpredictable.

That rapid evolution of the computer and chip industries demonstrate the need to be constantly aware of changes in the corporate environment. Think of companies like Polaroid and Kodak. Polaroid was once a member of the so-called "Nifty Fifty," a group of high-flying stocks that seemed like sure winners during the 1970's. Not long ago, Polaroid announced that it would cease making film for the cameras that once amazed customers by presenting fully developed photographs almost instantly. Kodak is another firm that has come under crushing pressure as it struggles to transform its film and camera business to the digital age.

Here's a quick review in bullet points of key criteria for stock screening:

- Consistent solid financial performance

- Consistently increasing distributed cash flow (Dividends)

- Real growth of the business over time. Companies should show evidence of real growth in the form of increasing cash flow and revenues per share over time.

- Return on shareholder equity greater than twice the risk-free rate of return of a 10 year treasury yield or a 10% return, whichever is greater

- Increasing cash flow per share over the past 5 years

- Increasing Revenues per share over the past 5 years

- Debt levels less than 40% of capitalization or debt levels below industry norms.

I want to get a reasonable rate of return from my equity holding over and above what I could have received if I had lent my money. For example, I know I can lend my money in the government bond market on a ten year basis and get a certain rate of return.

But if I am taking the risk of investing in the equity market, I want my return on shareholder equity to be at least twice what I would get if I were simply lending my money out by fixed income investing. That is the premium I require for taking the risk inherent in buying an equity compared to the security of something like a treasury bond.

Furthermore, I want that enhanced return on an equity holding each and every year going back for at least five years and every year going forward while I own the equity. Let us say that the yield on a ten year bond is four percent. I would expect at least an eight percent return on my equity. But that amount is still not enough because the history of the stock market shows a return of a little more than ten percent. This means that ten percent is really my true minimum. I also prefer to see a dividend rate that is sixty-five percent or less of cash flow because I am looking for fiscal sustainability. As I mentioned, companies do not pay out everything they make in cash flow in order to ensure that they can still afford to pay their dividend or increase it even if they have a rough year.

Finally we have identified an even smaller group of companies that fit our criteria. We believe they are fundamentally good businesses; they pay the dividends we want, they have a history of increasing their dividends, they have the cash flow to sustain dividend growth, and return on shareholder equity is ample.

The next challenge is to figure out an appropriate price for the businesses under consideration. If we can determine what a company is worth, then we know when a company is below fair value and therefore an attractive buy. By the same token, when a company's shares are trading above our target price they should be evaluated for sale.

To perform this crucial evaluation we use Earnings per Share as a key measure. And even though we do not use this in our stock screens, the market uses this measure to value stocks so we have to pay attention to it. We examine historical relationships between share prices and corporate earnings for each company.

Has the market not yet rewarded earnings increases with share price increases? We also need to know what a company's earnings are as predicted by a consensus of analysts who follow the company to be in the future.

Financial advisors use various tools for this corporate pricing calculation. Average investors can get the best compilation of this data on a twelve-year chart. Your financial advisor should have access to a number of more sophisticated tools to assess proper corporate valuation. The Securities Research Company (SRC) book provides charts going back as far as thirty-five years, but these are available by subscription only. I also like to use "Point and Figure" charts which provide different perspectives on stock price movement and something called a "Fundamental Valuation Sheet." This tool allows me to use the last ten years of fundamental data from a target company to create a relative valuation as well as discounted cash flow valuations.

It's a tricky, but crucially important task to set a fair market value on any given corporation, but that is the final key step in separating the wheat from the chaff among our stock picks.

Determining a company's fair value is a fluid activity that requires constant monitoring as circumstances change. For every company we determine the following price levels:

- The "Wish Buy Price": This is the level at which the company's value is compelling compared to historical levels

- The "Buyable Price": This is the level below which the company is considered buyable under our criteria

- The "Upside Evaluation Price": As values rise, this is the level of valuation at which an immediate revaluation of corporate value is performed

- The "Downside Evaluation Price": If stock prices decline, this is the level at which an immediate risk evaluation is performed.

- The "Long Term 'Get Out' Stop": This is the last support level at which we are willing to hold onto shares of a company.

My reasonable pricing methodology is really very simple from a fundamental standpoint. Every industry has different growth dynamics. For instance, a company in the high tech industry should grow at a much faster rate than a utility is going to grow. Therefore, each industry has a different Price-to-Earnings ratio at which its companies should trade. That's why I have to look at each company within its industry and how the market treats that industry as far as its P/E ratio is concerned.

We can't compare a high tech company to an oil company or a natural gas company. They have three completely different growth patterns, and the market is going to set the P/E ratios at which they will trade. As I said earlier, this is why I have to look at cash flow and profitability as well as P/E ratios in order to be looking at the same valuation metrics as the market.

My discipline is to look at the industry and the average P/E ratio for the companies in that industry as well as the average P/E ratio for an individual company. When a stock is trading at a discount to its normal P/E, it is probably in more of a buy range than a sell range. This is just common sense. The amount of the discount required to get my attention depends on the industry as well as the company within the industry. This is where my professional knowledge and experience as a portfolio manager is a great advantage.

I can see in my charts how the markets treat various companies when their earnings do different things. Obviously when a company trades at a premium P/E as compared to its normal P/E, then it is overvalued and subject to possible sale.

I would like to offer some crucial points for evaluating a company's fundamentals and its industry environment:

- S.W.O.T. Analysis – Identify the strengths, weaknesses, opportunities and any threats facing a business under consideration

- Credit Analysis – Crucial for companies that use leverage

- Industry Analysis – Determine if underlying industry has staying power. Keep in mind what happened to the computer business

- Competitor Analysis – Find out who the competitors are and decide if this the best business we could buy in this area

- Catalyst Evaluation – Determine which external events could cause upward or downward price movements within the next year.

One question I am frequently asked is whether or not I ever invest in companies that have no cash flow whatsoever. My answer is that sometimes there are companies that *seem* to have no cash flow. In reality they may be using cash flow internally because they are in the early phase of high growth when there is a lot of risk and expense in the execution of their business plan. There is also the risk that another company could take away part of their market share. The company in question may also face challenges in establishing its market share while trying to establish its brand as a household name. What is most important about cash flow in this kind of company is what they are doing with their revenues internally.

Let me give you a cautionary tale about a company that looked exceptional but had no cash flow. It is the story of an enterprise called Pacific Ethanol. Back in 2007 there was a presumption in government circles that federal tax dollars would be used to encourage the production of ethanol through subsidies as a partial solution to the energy crisis. The problem is that like almost all forms of alternative energy, you can't build an ethanol plant and have it operational overnight. There is a lot of lead time involved. It takes time to go through the permit process, to acquire the real estate, to develop proper engineering, and many other important considerations.

In spite of all the roadblocks, there were a number of companies all vying to become major manufacturers of ethanol. There was one in California known as Pacific Ethanol which had been around a long time before there was even any government backing. It was, however, started by businessmen who were connected to the government, mostly as former government officials.

In 2006 the company had been the darling of the financial press because some of its key people were known to be from the investment arm of Microsoft, and they were planning to invest in Pacific Ethanol. After the influx of cash from Microsoft executives, the company went from the low teens to forty dollars per share. This was in spite of the fact that it had no production facilities up and running even though they had plans for five plants. It would have been at least three years before a single drop of ethanol would have come out of one of those plants.

What's more, the company didn't have any contracts with the suppliers of the raw material which was supposed to be converted to ethanol. In fact the only thing they did have was an impressive looking business plan. Yet the stock, which started in single digits, wound up at $44 per share merely on the expectation of what was going to happen in the future.

There was not a single dollar of cash flow behind this company. Even worse, the cash flow was negative because Pacific Ethanol was burning through its funds. So no matter how great the idea sounded, investing didn't make any sense at the price people were willing to pay for the company.

Although I never bought any shares of Pacific Ethanol for my clients or for my mutual fund, I had several clients who did so on their own. As soon as I heard about their investment I advised them to sell their holdings. Only one client listened and sold his stock in the high twenties. Obviously he was not very happy with me when the stock went to forty dollars a share, but he thanked me profusely when it fell back into the teens.

Today the stock is still well under ten dollars a share, and I still have clients who are waiting for it to come back. The problem is that Pacific Ethanol has become what I call a "show me" stock. And without cash flow it will probably never recover even a portion of its former luster. This is the same scenario that happened to those who invested in the high tech bubble of Silicon Valley and the early investors in biotech which didn't promise any cash flow for at least ten years down the road.

What about selling our holdings? No matter how carefully and successfully we have chosen companies to invest in, the time will come when we need to sell some of these positions. Making a sell decision can sometimes be a subjective call. But there are certain triggers and criteria that should make every investor think about selling.

- Companies that no longer meet the screening criteria

- Market value of the investor's position exceeds 10% of the portfolio (sell a portion of the holding)

- Too much concentration of a portfolio in an industry or sub industry. (sell a portion of the holding)

- Excessive concentration in a single sector of the economy. 25% in any sector is the maximum that I recommend

- If greater value exists elsewhere, sell your weakest holding and buy the better value

- If a company has dropped below our long term "Get Out" stop price

- When a stock reaches its' target price, and it is overvalued, a trailing stop order is entered.

Raising the price of a stop-sell order in tandem with the price of a rising stock is what a "trailing stop" is all about. A "trailing stop" is a safety valve that I use to avoid selling a company prematurely when it is rising in value. There are specific disciplines to trailing stops. First of all, *once a stop is placed, it is never removed.* This is because you should never reconsider the fact that you put in the stop. *And once a stop is placed, you can raise the price of the stop, but you can never lower it.* In fact, periodically you must raise the price of the stop.

I do this manually each and every night with all my stocks based on the last trade of the day. I never use the intra day basis because in today's highly volatile market some stocks get whipsawed so much during just a few hours that I could get stopped out when I don't want that to happen.

I have evaluation points that lead to sales or stops. This means that if a stock that I or a client owns rises to a particular price, then this is a cue for me to evaluate it to find out if I want to put a trailing stop in or just sell. Perhaps enough time has passed holding this rising stock that the sell range should have been raised anyway. That means it is actually in the hold range now because when I put that stop price on at the last evaluation point, two years may have passed. In the meantime earnings may have gone up so the sell price is no longer valid. It could be twenty points higher now.

The first step is to always take the time to do an evaluation. And if that shows a stock is overvalued, then I put in a stop loss order, or a sell. In order to create trailing stops, technical analysis comes into play. Technical analysis is a special discipline unto itself. I will not try to go through all of its fine points here; suffice it to say that enough market participants follow the disciplines for them to be observed and paid attention to when making short term timing decisions. I will look at the appropriate chart when I make an evaluation and decide if there is support on the downside at a certain price. This support is a point where enough investors have previously purchased the stock that there will be resistance to its dropping below that price level. This way I can go just below that point. If the price starts to freefall from there, I am out of that stock before it can trend down to the next support level.

I review all stock prices on a regular basis. If a particular stock has moved higher, I will reevaluate it to see if I want to raise the stop. If a stock starts to plateau, at a certain point, it will be stopped out because it has failed my discipline which requires that it continue to rise.

Sometimes a stock goes up and right back down again before I have a chance to sell. This is what I call "round-tripping a trade", and it's obviously something to avoid. As I have said, when a stock reaches its target price, I want to have established trailing stop points well in advance. In other words, once a stock reaches the target price at which I feel it is overvalued, I don't want to lose the gain I have just achieved. Normally I would have sold the stock or placed a stop-sell order trailing just behind the new high water mark.

Here are the key points governing stop disciplines:

- Once a stop order is placed it is never removed

- A stop-sell order can be raised but never lowered

- Stop-sell order limits should be evaluated weekly for potential increases, trailing the price of a rising stock.

Many investors make the mistake of hesitating before selling a stock. Surprisingly enough, I have found that many investors are often quick and impulsive about buying equities when they have positive feelings about a particular company. Strangely, these same investors will frequently drag their heels before selling an underperforming stock.

It's a phenomenon that has never been well explained. It is possible that investors do not want to acknowledge that they have made a poor buying decision by selling an underperforming stock. Some investors do not want to absorb the losses that come with selling a money-losing investment. And sometimes there is simply an emotional attachment which prevents an investor from taking the necessary step to cut his losses.

Selling is just as important as buying in the rapidly-changing world of equities. Many times there are warning signs that can arouse our suspicions before bad news appears in an earnings report. If we can spot the warning signs early enough, we can sell our holdings of a potentially troubled company before share prices plunge.

These are the key areas to keep watch for early warning signs:

- Cash Flow: If cash flow per share is declining, sell the position

- Debt Increases: If debt is rising, be wary but don't panic. The company may be taking on debt in order to make a new acquisition. As long as the debt is being paid down, your investment may still be safe

- Return on Shareholder Equity (ROSE): If ROSE drops below acceptable levels, sell the stock.

Don't hesitate to sell a company that displays any of these warning signs. The company will continue in whatever direction it was headed with or without you. But there's no need for you, the investor, to go down with a sinking ship.

And, don't worry about finding a replacement. There are many companies that meet or exceed our rigorous criteria for picking equity investments. There's no reason to hold on to investments in companies that don't make the grade.

REAL ESTATE

Although almost everyone owns equities, real estate is perhaps the most overlooked investment by financial advisors when they construct portfolios for their clients. I advocate putting one-third of your money into real estate and other asset based investments for two reasons. First of all they are designed to provide an inflation hedge and a cash flow that should increase with inflation. In addition, they have proven over market cycles that they are non-correlated to equities and fixed income. When bonds or stocks are falling, real estate should be bucking the trend. This tendency should substantially reduce the overall volatility of your portfolio.

There is and always has been a great deal of confusion over real estate. This stems from the fact that most people confuse the value of their house with the value of real estate as an investment. Let me clear up the confusion by stating categorically that your house is not investment real estate. Houses are an expense. You not only have to pay off a mortgage, you have to pay off the interest associated with it. There are also property taxes that have to be paid every year as well as insurance. On top of this you are confronted with ongoing repairs and the cost of basic utilities. In spite of these expenses, you have probably built up some degree of equity in your home. This may lead you to think of your home as an asset. But while you may think of it as an asset, it is not because it does not fit the basic definition of an asset, which is something that creates positive cash flow.

In addition, if you look at the value of a house purchased right after World War II, you will see that after all the expenses it probably hasn't even kept up with inflation. There is only one instance in which houses become an asset. That is when they become rental properties with the rents producing cash flow to the owner. This is not to say you should not invest in a home. You do, after all, need some place to live. And there is the real advantage of having a fixed housing expense and allowing it to get relatively cheaper every year as inflation raises the cost of rent for those who do not own their own homes. But this does mean you shouldn't depend on your residence to serve as the real estate component of your asset allocation. For purposes of asset allocation the only true investment quality real estate is commercial real estate.

One problem that many investors have is that investing in commercial real estate is completely off most people's radar. Even though taken as a whole it is a major asset class, it is seldom, if ever, reported on by the financial press. What has been making daily headlines in all the news of 2008 is the mortgage meltdown. Unfortunately this coverage makes all real estate seem dicey at best. You have to remember that the scary news about the government takeover of Fannie Mae and Freddie Mac is predominately about residential real estate and mortgages. And if this news causes you to stay away from commercial properties, then you are missing out on a critical asset class that can bring you rewards and portfolio stability that no other asset class can.

Another problem is that Wall Street, as well as most financial advisors, tend to ignore commercial real estate as a viable investment. They are and always have been fixated on stocks and bonds. While this asset class is second only to fixed income as far as invested dollars, the market capitalization of publically traded real estate mutual funds is very small when compared to the market capitalization of publically traded corporations. The great preponderance of commercial real estate is directly owned and not owned in publicly traded liquid securities. This means you need to be somewhat self-educated when it comes to investing in real estate, but it need not be intimidating. You don't have to be a multimillionaire or know someone in the industry to participate. And you certainly don't have to buy an entire office building or apartment complex. You can own commercial real estate by buying only a proportional share.

Although some investors participate in commercial real estate by buying properties directly, trading in it can be as easy as buying a stock and give you the same liquidity but with a predictable cash flow. There are basically two instruments that let you buy a proportional share of a property or portfolio of properties. These are REITs and REIT mutual funds. While these securities are traded like stocks, they carry important differences, particularly with regard to tax treatment.

A REIT or Real Estate Investment Trust is simply a company that owns and manages income-producing real estate. REITs were created by an act of Congress in the 1970s to enable large and small investors alike to enjoy the rental income from commercial property. They also served the purpose of enabling those people who wanted to build large commercial properties with the means to secure funding from a large number of sources. Although they went through some hard times with poorly structured deals that caused a negative reaction on Wall Street, most survived.

There are many benefits associated with owning a REIT. REITs must comply with very strict government guidelines. The most important of these is that they must distribute at least ninety percent of their taxable income to shareholders each year as dividends or they will lose their status. Fortunately this means a REIT is permitted to deduct dividends paid to shareholders from its taxable income. The government also requires that a REIT hold at least seventy-five percent of its assets in real estate, cash and government securities. Their dividends are generally secured by stable rents from long term leases. These rules should serve to give shareholders a great measure of security about the reliability of their cash flow.

For many investors the main attraction of a REIT is its high dividend yield. However, the average long term or fifteen year yield on a REIT is eight percent. While this is well above the yield of the S&P Index every year, it does not meet my preferred investment criterion of ten percent. Therefore, you must search for REITs that meet my criteria for buy disciplines. This means you need to pay special attention to my buy disciplines for REITs which I outline later on in the chapter.

Since REIT shares are bought and sold on a stock exchange, they are easily traded and have great liquidity. Of course there is the downside that by being so liquid, these shares are also subject to the emotional mispricings that occasionally happen to publicly traded shares. By contrast, if you were to buy and sell property directly, you would have to pay much higher expenses. In addition your real estate transactions would most likely take a great deal of time and require much effort.

As well as high liquidity, owning REITs gives diversification to an investment portfolio. As I have said, they are a perfect component of your asset allocation because they increase your returns while reducing your risk due to their lack of correlation to the S&P. However, if interest rates go up, money could flow out of REITs and into fixed income. At least if the price of their shares goes down, you are still provided a reliable cash flow. That alone is worth a great deal.

Many of the Real Estate Investment Trusts follow the long term pattern I like. They have increasing cash flows because most of their long term leases have inflation clauses in them. When rents go up, cash flow goes up. More people will then pay for the higher cash flow, so the real estate goes up in value. Over the very long term both your principal in real estate and your income should go up with inflation.

 When you consider buying REITs, you will see that the different sectors are divided by the type of real estate they hold as well as the duration of the leases. Be aware that every type of building has different economics associated with it. Although REITs specialize by property types, the largest proportion invests in offices.

One big advantage to owning office buildings is that they require a relatively long lease of three years or more with options to extend. If your REIT is comprised of office buildings, not only do you have long term, stable tenants, you know that they are required to give at least six months' notice before vacating. This means there should be plenty of time to find new occupants before the old ones are gone. Because offices have long lease times with predictable cash flows, they tend to trade at a higher price or lower yield.

If we are considering different categories of office buildings, they can be broken up into office buildings in metropolitan areas and those in small markets. They may be office buildings that house a large number of tenants or office buildings that are sale lease backs for corporate headquarters. This category of real estate is known as a triple net lease. What this means to you as investor is that the owner of the building does not need to worry about covering all the expenses, all he has to do is collect the check. Another major category of REITs is the kind that invests in government office buildings. In short, the universe of office buildings alone is gigantic.

REITs also invest in sectors including shopping centers, apartment complexes, discount malls, industrial facilities, hotels, self-storage units, health care facilities, entertainment complexes, timberlands, condo conversions, mobile home parks, and marinas. The first of my REIT buy disciplines is to maintain industry diversification as represented by a variety of property types. The third of your model portfolio that is devoted to real estate should maintain a minimum of at least five positions and not more than twenty within the allocation. Remember each REIT is in itself a diversified portfolio so that is why you can have as few as five REIT's in a portfolio and not ten.

When considering buying a REIT, you need to realize they operate just like stocks. At any point in time some sectors are overvalued, and some are undervalued. As a money manager who uses REITs in my clients' portfolios, I am constantly evaluating them. With REITs I don't have at my disposal as great a number of statistical screening methods as I do with stocks. Therefore I use my own metrics associated with REITs. These have to do with funds from operations, which is the reported annual cash flow. I expect to see funds from operation rise each year, and I do expect to see dividends increasing over time. Of course that dividend yield should always be in excess of a ten year treasury.

As I do with my equity investments, I first go through a statistical screening to reduce the number of REITs under consideration. I begin to see what looks overvalued and what looks undervalued. Then I look at each individual company to see if it is one I want to own. With REITs I pay very close attention to the management and their expertise within the REIT sector. Sometimes a management team looks great, but on closer inspection, I see that one of the chief managers is no longer there. With management you are buying past performance and industry contacts, so you need to carefully scrutinize the remaining team. I cannot emphasize enough how important the consistency of management is when buying real estate.

It is important to examine a REIT's debt load to make sure your potential investment is not over-leveraged. I prefer to buy REITs that are valued below their liquidation net asset value. That's a good way of staying clear of REITs that carry too much debt.

But the most important criterion is a REIT's funds from operation ratio. It is the closest equivalent to a commercial property's capitalization rate, or Cap Rate for short. In the simplest terms, a Cap Rate is the real estate world's equivalent of a stock's P/E ratio. If the number is too low, the asset is overvalued.

The capitalization rate for any property is determined by dividing the property's net operating income by its purchase price. Generally, high cap rates indicate higher returns and greater perceived risk. The same yardstick can be applied by REIT managers to the value of their stable of properties and the net income those properties generate. For instance, if a property has a 5% cap rate, that means it returns 5% of its purchase price as return on investment. By this yardstick, if it is a property worth $1,000,000 it should return $50,000 a year after covering expenses.

While most investors consider stocks with high P/E ratios to be especially risky, REITs and real estate investments are priced on Capitalization Rates (Cap Rates), and generally the higher the Cap Rate, the lower the risk. As I said earlier, low cap rates are considered potentially overpriced. A stock will have a high

PE when everything is working well at the company and the investing public takes note of that success and believes it will continue into the future. The same goes for Real Estate when it has a low Cap Rate. However, there are some correlations between the cap rates that buildings will trade at and indications of how well they are managed, or the length of their leases. For example, property being sold at a 5% cap rate is often characterized by low vacancy rates, good management, and strong cash flow from rents because the property is perceived to be operating at its full potential. This property's value is greater because of its excellent performance, so a higher price is asked by the seller. The higher selling price makes the cap rate lower. This is the kind of property any investor would prefer; however, they have to pay a premium price to get such stable fundamentals (hence a low yield on their investment, or low Cap Rate).

By contrast, a property being sold at a 10% cap rate may have a higher vacancy rate, shorter leases, and fewer amenities. The property value would obviously be lower, and that fact would tend to drive the cap rate up in order to make it more attractive to a potential investor.

The cap rate operates very much like the relationship between a bond yield and the value of the bond. If interest rates rise, the value of a bond will decline. By the same token, when the cap rate goes up, the value of the property has gone down (assuming the cash flow from that property remains the same).

Cap rates are a function of the perceived risk of capital and also the cost of obtaining the mortgage money. If the cost of borrowing money to buy real estate goes up, then the yield the property must generate will have to rise to offset that increased borrowing cost. Given that many real estate transactions are done with a substantial amount of borrowed money, the cost of that mortgage money can be one of the greatest determining factors as to the pricing of the real estate itself. When there is substantial mortgage money available and lenders are competing to make loans, then one would expect the interest rates to come down. When mortgage interest rates come down, the Cap Rate can come down. When the Cap Rate goes down, the value of the property has clearly risen, assuming again the rental income has remained the same. Of course the opposite is also true. When mortgage interest rates increase, so will cap rates, and then the values of the buildings will decline. Cap Rates can provide a useful yardstick when buying REITs or revenue-producing properties directly.

While buying REITs in order to own a share of the commercial real estate market can be appealing but daunting, there is another option. You can buy a REIT mutual fund as all or part of the real estate component of your portfolio. Certainly the manager of a mutual fund that specializes in REITs will be much more knowledgeable about the industry and all its sectors and subsectors than the average investor. They also should be aware of what is a reasonable amount of leverage and the trends in lending activity. Another factor in determining how well a REIT or REIT mutual fund is managed is recognizing that good management does not simply consist of ongoing management of the properties involved. At times some of the properties will need to be bought or sold so you need someone who is an expert in the acquisition as well as sales of the properties involved.

Another advantage of the mutual fund approach is that the minimum amount of money required to invest can be very small. There are funds that require only $250, but $2,000 or more is the norm. The capital barriers to purchasing an individual property are very high. It would take huge amounts of capital to acquire a diversified portfolio of properties. For the investor with more limited amounts of capital to invest in this asset class, individual REITs or a mutual fund may be the only effective way to invest. To build a portfolio of individual REITs with a limited amount of capital also might be difficult to accomplish, and the transaction costs may be prohibitive. In addition to increased diversity, REIT mutual funds provide financial statements that help you keep current with your investments and assist you with tax preparation.

There are two types of mutual funds in existence: Open end and Closed end funds. Both are diversified portfolios that are professionally managed on a daily basis. The difference is in how they are purchased and sold. An open end fund will have shares available to be purchased every day at the Net Asset Value of the portfolio of investments. And if you wish to sell your shares, they will be redeemed at the Net Asset Value of the portfolio at the end of the day of redemption. Closed end funds have a set number of shares in existence and if you want to buy shares, you must buy them form somebody who wishes to sell their shares. The fund itself does not redeem your shares for their value. Because there is a traded market in the shares, they can trade for a price different from what the portfolio is worth or the portfolio's Net Asset Value. If they are trading below the NAV, then they are trading at a discount to the portfolio value. If they are trading above the NAV then they are trading at a premium. Again common sense is your guide. Generally you want to buy the funds you like when they are trading at a discount and sell them when they trade at a premium. Remember that the funds you choose should offer a competitive dividend advantage and be purchased at a discount to Net Asset Value.

While some clients may prefer the ease and liquidity of REITs and REIT mutual funds to provide an inflation hedge and a cash flow that should increase with inflation, those clients who invest directly and use prudent leverage, find there is the greater potential for wealth creation in direct ownership of real estate assets. Unfortunately as an asset class real estate is particularly vulnerable to get rich quick schemes. But if you follow my disciplines at the end of this chapter, you should not fall prey to most of these.

If you decide to buy commercial property outside of a REIT or a REIT mutual fund, you need to do this in consultation with many people. However, first of all you need to look at your own cash flow situation. For instance, if you are thinking of purchasing a strip mall, you need to know if you could survive financially if you lose a tenant for a period of time.

Next you should consult with your CPA to find out if the tax benefits associated with personal ownership are of any real value to you. You also need to talk to lawyers who are conversant in the field of real estate to find out what kind of ownership is most beneficial. Do you want a Limited Liability Corporation, a Limited Partnership, or a Family Partnership? Or perhaps you want to own it personally. In general people want to segregate their real estate so it does not affect the rest of their financial picture.

Then you need to delve into other considerations. As I list just a few of them here, you will see the need for a reputable and competent Real Estate Broker to guide you. Depending on the type of real estate, you may need a property manager. Does he need to be on or offsite and full or part time? What will he cost to hire? What are the maintenance issues involved with the property you are considering, and do you have the expertise to handle them? How old is the building? Could there be asbestos abatement issues which can more than double your repair costs should the building require work in the future? Are there groundwater issues? Is the rebar intact or rusting? Obviously you need to have a highly qualified inspector along with all the original plans plus the paperwork regarding the repairs over the years.

Zoning, entitlements, and taxation are huge considerations. I have just scratched the surface of the list. There is a multitude of considerations that go into the purchase and management of commercial real estate. If you are planning to do it yourself, you practically need to be a professional in the industry. This is the reason I usually steer clients away from buying commercial property directly. However there is one exception to this, and that applies to my clients who are small business owners.

One way many Americans have become direct owners of commercial real estate and use leverage properly is through starting a small business and buying the property it is located on at the same time.

Say, for example, you buy a laundromat on Main Street in January. You don't just buy the business; you buy the building as well. You might hire somebody to run the laundromat for you and watch the great cash flow that comes in from the operating business. As time goes on and you grow your business, your cash flow should increase. You might be able to charge fifteen cents more for every shirt you press during the second year you own the business while your expenses have grown by only five cents. The extra ten cents on every shirt flows to you, the owner. You are following your plan of buying a business and continuing to own it over time with increasing cash flow, some of which pays down your mortgage.

As you continue to plough more money back into the laundromat every year and your cash flow grows, the value of your business would increase as well. Now there might be a point in time after you have owned the laundromat that it has become extremely valuable because a new apartment development has been built next door with no laundry facilities. People are now pounding down your door to buy your business because of its incredible cash flow. You could sell and take the money to buy another type of business that is underutilized in your marketplace. Perhaps it is a tire store.

You know it is time to do this because you have grown your laundromat to encompass a ninety percent share of the available market, leaving it very little room to grow still further. On the other hand, the tire store has only a ten percent share which gives you lots of upside. Remember also that when you bought the laundromat, you were smart enough to buy the building as well. Suppose that over the course of a few years you have been able to pay down the mortgage on the building, and you wind up owning it free and clear. Part of the benefit of buying that building is that the new owner of the laundromat, whoever that might be, owes the building rent, and the proceeds from that rent are ultimately greater than the cost of the purchase of the building. That rent represents ongoing cash flow. This is just one example of how real estate can work for you.

You know enough to buy the building as well as the business when you purchase the tire store. Again you structure things so your business covers the mortgage payments plus something extra. Even if the tire store goes under, the new business that replaces it will still have to pay rent to you, the owner of the property.

 If you own a piece of real estate, you are probably going to own it longer than you will own the business because it is a cash cow. Again, once the mortgage is paid off, you own a wonderful net positive steady stream of income.

A lot of wealth in America has been created by businesses building up asset values in the form of commercial real estate ownership. So your portfolio should be doing the same thing.

What you are doing is diversifying your assets by owning both the business and the real estate. If you had a cash reserve in the bank for this business, then you are living the principles I espouse of owning stocks in the form of the business real estate in the form of the building the business is in, and fixed income in the form of the cash reserves! However, at times fear spreads across the real estate marketplace. This can be a great opportunity to buy more of your real estate asset class. After all, you want to buy an asset class when it is low and sell it when it is high. That is what rebalancing is all about.

The big difference is that the commercial real estate pays cash flow in terms of rent and even though real estate may go through a bad market cycle, the cash flow is not going to change much. In fact, the leases on the properties may extend well past the market cycle. Furthermore, the benefit of compounding that you can see in the equities markets also works in the commercial real estate market and comprises the bulk of the growth of your total investment.

Real estate and equities are remarkably similar because they are both ways to own assets as opposed to fixed income investing. Remarkably, if you look at the total rate of return on both equities and commercial real estate since World War II, they are within one percent per year of each other. The amazing thing is that they are countercyclical. As I said in the beginning, they have a negative correlation, which means that when one goes up, the other goes down.

For example, in March of 2000, the stock market peaked. People were taking money out of real estate to put into the stock market because they believed Internet stocks were going through the roof. But, as you know, the stock market started going down, and real estate was soon perceived again as a safer investment. During this period, interest rates were dropping and this made real estate even more attractive. As interest rates go down, bonds offer lower returns also, so the cash flow from commercial real estate becomes even more valuable and desirable. In short, real estate often goes up in value when stocks and interest rates are going down.

This hopefully illustrates to you why you want to own real estate in addition to owning stocks. It is an asset which pays you a dividend in the form of rent much like the dividends from stocks and the yields of bonds. And if that rent is reinvested either by paying down the mortgage or by buying more real estate, you are going to compound your real estate assets over time. These assets are roughly equal to owning a business. Real estate can also outpace inflation. If your real estate holdings are leveraged to any degree, the positive cash flow generated by your holdings should support both the leverage and the other expenses of real estate ownership.

Sometimes I have a hard time convincing my clients to buy commercial real estate. They are afraid of it because it is underemployed as an investment tool and can be complex to understand. I hope by reading this chapter, real estate has become demystified for you and its unique advantages make it worth a portion of your investment dollar.

FIXED INCOME INVESTING

When I buy fixed income assets for clients, I am buying the preservation of their capital and the predictable cash flow they produce. If I adhere to my rule of investing one third of a portfolio in each asset class, fixed income investing lowers the volatility of a client's total portfolio substantially. And if fixed assets are properly structured, even during periods of economic downturns and down market cycles, they will also provide liquidity without having to sell temporarily depreciated assets should my clients have a need for principal.

The problem I see frequently in my practice is that many people are averse to fixed income investing, particularly bonds. I was working with a lady, and I suggested she needed some municipal bonds in her portfolio within her taxable account because ultimately she could improve the yield on her investments. All her friends had convinced her to stay away from fixed income by telling her it doesn't provide any growth. But as we continued our discussion, I discovered she had CDs at two different banks. One was a five year CD, and one was a two year CD. Therefore she effectively had a five year bond and a two year bond.

The real reason she was partial to her CDs is that they gave her FDIC insurance. As we talked, I convinced her that there were two municipalities that were in such great financial shape that they had set aside money in U.S. Treasury obligations to pay off the bonds when they were redeemable. These were direct obligations of the federal government which were an even stronger guarantee than FDIC insurance. On top of that her CDs with each bank exceeded the $100,000 insurance limit. Ultimately she wound up acquiring the municipal bonds and did not have to pay tax on the income they produced.

My client had also purchased CDs because they seemed to be easy and safe way to invest. The problem is that they have a hard time keeping up with inflation. In general CD returns are based on the length of time that a depositor is willing to lock up his money. The longer the time period, the higher the return. While you will eventually get all your money plus interest back, you will be penalized for early withdrawal.

Be sure to ask your financial advisor before locking up any of your assets in CDs. He may well have other fixed income financial instruments that will equal the security of CDs and give you some measure of inflation protection as well.

The most common form of fixed income investing is, of course, bonds. A bond is simply a loan for which you get an IOU in return. That IOU may have many different names: Certificate of Deposit (CD), Bond, Debenture, Mortgage, Note, Bill, Collateralized Mortgage Obligation (CMO), Money Market, or

Commercial Paper to name a few. For simplicity we will refer to fixed income instruments as bonds, as they are a contractual bond between you the lender and the borrower. Just as you would insist on repayment terms any time you lend money, you need to do the same with bonds. The terms you will need to consider when investing in bonds are:

- The yield or coupon rate: what interest rate will the issuer of the bond pay you on your investment?

- The maturity: When must you be repaid your original principal?

- The payment schedule: How often and on what dates will you receive your interest payments?

- Value: What is the value of the bond at the time of purchase and what will it be at maturity?

- Quality: What is the credit rating of the bond issuer?

- What underlying assets or security is there to provide repayment should things change.

Security of principal is paramount over the long term. I will therefore give up a small amount of yield for the safety of the principal. Should I ever take a position in something that is not very highly rated, it will only be after significant research with fundamental value backing up the debt.

Although I have described a bond investment as a loan, there is a simple reason why people talk about buying a bond rather than making a loan. Bonds are traded by brokers on the open market like stocks or other forms of tradable securities. The value of a bond when it is traded is primarily affected by its yield, its maturity date, and its credit rating and to a lesser extent, things like liquidity, the size of the issue, and its taxable status.

When a bond is originally issued, the yield is heavily influenced by the prevailing interest rates at the time it is issued. There are many factors that influence the yield when the bond is issued. Some of these factors are where we are in the economic cycle, where the Federal Reserve has set interest rates, and what the inflation rate is. As a general rule, the better the economy is doing, the higher interest rates will be. It is when the economy is poor that the Federal Reserve will inject money into the system and lower interest rates. The other major factor that affects the yield is the creditworthiness of the bond issuer. If a company or municipality already has a significant amount of debt on its balance sheet and is not showing enough cash flow to service that debt, then obviously the credit rating will be low. Those municipalities or corporations that in reality do not need to borrow the money or have ample cash flow to pay the borrowings back, will sell highly rated bonds. There are companies that will analyze the credit worthiness of bond issuers and those credit ratings will impact the interest rate the issuer has to pay to borrow the money. The issuer with a low credit rating will be forced to pay a much higher interest rate to attract investors. Obviously an investor gets paid more to take on more risk of default. The real question is how much risk should one take on to get a little bit higher rate of interest.

Bond yields are also affected by the maturity or length of time before the owner must by repaid. It is often assumed that long term bonds pay higher yields than short term bonds, having to pay the lender of the money a premium for locking their money up for a longer period of time. But, this is not always true. There are periods of time when the short term rates are higher than longer term rates. This is described as a period of an inverted yield curve. Generally these periods of time do not last for very long and are at times when there are disruptions in the economy.

Certainly the best thing about having bonds as part of your portfolio is that they provide a steady and dependable cash flow. Bonds generally pay much more than bank CDs, and they certainly outpace some stock dividends. Also, without question good quality bonds are safe if held to maturity. But the market value of a bond will probably fluctuate no matter how sound the credit rating of the borrower.

The market value is determined in the marketplace every day according to the prevailing interest rates for comparable maturities. Let me give you an example of how this works and how it can affect you.

Let's say a bond is issued with a face value of $10,000 and with a 5% interest rate yield. If interest rates rise, the face value of your bond will go down. While this sounds odd, it really is just common sense. In a higher interest rate environment bonds must increase their yield in order to stay competitive. Let's assume that after the interest rate hike bonds are now being issued with a 6% yield. If you are now trying to sell your 5% bond at its original face value of $10,000, no one would want to buy it.

In order to sell a bond that is generating lower returns than the competition (the new bonds that are being issued at a higher interest rate), you must discount its price. Buyers of your bond will demand compensation for its lower returns, and the size of the discount you must give will be set according to the current interest rate for bonds of similar quality and maturity. The amount of that discount will become larger the more interest rates rise.

Conversely, a drop in interest rates can make your bond more valuable. As an example let us suppose you own a $10,000 bond that is generating a 7% yield, and interest rates for corporate bonds have fallen to 5%. If you decide to sell, you could get a great deal more than the amount you paid for your bond. The downside would be that in selling your bond you are also giving up a good cash flow from that bond.

Most people don't buy and sell bonds for speculation but for the security and the stability of their income. A skilled professional can help you structure your bond holdings so that you are much less likely to be forced into a situation where you have to sell your bonds at a loss. This is done by using a technique called laddering. It can help you reduce risk while increasing the stability and predictability of your financial future. My rule of thumb is that you should have enough money maturing each year to take care of a year's worth of expenses.

When structuring a bond ladder, you will be looking for bonds with different maturity dates depending on your needs for liquidity. For most investors the object is to create a series of bonds which mature periodically one after the other. Each maturity date is thought of as a rung on the ladder.

I believe in starting to ladder bonds while a person is still in his twenties. So you would build up a one year maturity to cover your annual expenses; then you move on and build up a two year maturity. The idea is that when the one year bond matures, you ask yourself if you really need the money. If you don't, then you use the money to buy another bond at the end of your maturity schedule. This is how you build out a laddered portfolio from scratch.

There are several charts that show the trend of interest rates moves lasts for decades. As I write this book, we have had an almost thirty year move in interest rates. But what about the future? If you feel that the next move in interest rates will be up rather than down, there is a way to take advantage of this trend in a fixed income portfolio while hedging against inflation. Buy bonds with maturities designed to roll over on a short term basis. This way as they roll over, you will get ever higher interest rates and increase the cash flow of the fixed income portion of your portfolio. You probably want bonds with a maturity of five years or less in order to do this.

When you think interest rates are going down, there will still be some bonds that will continue to pay at higher than market rates for a significant period of time. Owning these should give you some piece of mind. In a low interest rate environment the equities portion of your asset allocation should give you increased returns causing that portion of your asset allocation to grow. Then when you rebalance your portfolio, you have an opportunity to buy more bonds at a lower price. This will give you additional interest income or cash flow.

If you feel that you are in a normal environment and buying a fixed income ladder, how do you know how long you should have as your longest maturity in your laddered portfolio? Again we are going to use some common sense and a picture to get the answer. First let's look at the picture. When we described the concept that the longer you committed your money, the higher the interest rate should be, this concept can be plotted on a graph. The interest rate would be on the up and down axis and the length of time to maturity would be on the horizontal axis. As you plot the various maturities and interest rates you are plotting what is known as the "Yield Curve". It is easy to look at this graph and see when the incremental additional years of length of maturity do not give you additional rates of return. This point on this graph is where the yield curve "flattens out". In a normal environment that point is going to be somewhere between seven to ten years. When you can not get paid additional interest for committing your money long term, you should not invest past that point in bonds. Therefore it follows that in a normal environment you want a seven to ten year ladder.

Another reason for this length of time for a bond ladder is that most investors want enough bonds to take them through a market cycle in equities. Should they happen to invest in equities at the top of a market cycle, history has shown that being able to hold those equities for five years or more should be enough time to see them rise again. By going out 7 to 10 years you are giving yourself more than enough time to ride a cycle in equities. You would buy a mixture of short and medium term bonds with maturity dates that fall once a year every year for the entire seven year period. Believe me, when we are in a free fall in stock prices, most of my clients are deliriously happy that they own bonds because that is a portion of their portfolio that they see has not gone down and they know can fund their lifestyle until the markets turn around and recover. It gives them the patience to allow their equities to work through bad market cycles. They can use the cash flow for living expenses, to buy more assets if they are in the accumulation stage, or they can use bonds to rebalance their portfolio. Keep in mind that between January of 2006 and August of 2008, the total return on bonds was better than the return on the stock market. Unfortunately, most investors don't realize that bonds can outperform the equity markets for periods of time. That makes them a wonderful hedge against volatility on Wall Street.

Many of my clients are not only wary of bonds: they also don't want to purchase bonds with maturities as long as seven to ten years. The problem is that they are not looking at their probable lifetime. A sixty year-old person most likely has over twenty years to live. If they buy bonds with a seven year ladder, that ladder is going to completely roll over at least three times before they die.

So buying a seven year ladder is quite sensible for someone who is sixty years old. The benefits of doing so are huge for your liquidity needs, for your rebalancing needs, and you don't have to worry about whether you are buying at a premium or a discount because your bonds will always mature at par.

Of course you should always be looking to get the best yield on your portfolio with the shortest duration. Although it sounds amazing, if you buy a ten year laddered portfolio, it will actually have a duration of less than five years. The duration is a highly complex calculation best left to professionals in which they figure out the average length of time for your portfolio to return your principal to you. This calculation takes into account the average maturity length of your bonds as well as the cash flow that accrues. Because bonds have a cash flow coming in on a regular basis, the interest is constantly compounding to such a degree that it greatly shortens the average maturity. This means that even though you may be buying longer term bonds, the pricing volatility is lowered to a considerably shorter period than the maturity of the bond.

If you use these strategies, a predetermined amount of your principal that is devoted to the fixed income portion of your asset allocation model will be available to you every year as cash flow. The chances are therefore much smaller that you will be forced to sell bonds before their maturity to generate the cash you need. As I've said, selling bonds before maturity can result in loss of principal. If they are laddered and held to maturity, bonds are redeemed for the full face value of their original purchase price.

While laddering is an effective strategy to safeguard your principal, it is not a perfect solution because you will still be affected by the fluctuations of rising and falling interest rates should you choose to reinvest rather than using the cash flow. For instance, if your bond matures and interest rates have fallen, the income stream from any new bond you buy will be lower.

There is another problem that could disrupt the careful laddering plan you have created. Watch out when you buy a bond that it is "callable." A bond issuer may decide to call back a bond if interest rates have dropped considerably. This is because it makes simple economic sense to the issuer to buy back his bond and issue a new series of securities at lower interest rates. It is much like refinancing a mortgage on your home to capture lower interest rates; good for the borrower but not so attractive to the lender. Even though you will be paid the full face value of your bond, this will play havoc with what is supposed to be the cash flow you expected to get from that bond. The question is how do you know if a bond is callable? A callable bond must always list the dates when the issuer can redeem his bonds and the information is available when you are buying a bond from the dealer who is selling it to you.

As mentioned earlier, one of the most important considerations when buying bonds is their quality. Bonds that are backed by the United States government are considered about as safe as you can get when held to the date of maturity. If you are considering the purchase of bonds for the short term, in other words for one year or less, you can't find anything safer than Treasury Bills or

T-bills. These can be bought for terms as short as three months on new issues and as short as a day on the secondary markets.

If you need to purchase absolute safety for the intermediate term, then you will want to consider Treasury notes. These have an initial maturity between two and ten years. Above ten years and stretching out to thirty years, your choice would be Treasury Bonds. Just like T-Bills, these can be purchased on the secondary market for lengths of time that are much shorter.

Aside from safety, there are definite advantages to buying Treasuries. First of all most of these bonds are not callable so you can ladder them without fear of your cash flow being disrupted. Also, if you happen to live in a state that levies income tax, the income from your Treasury bonds will not be taxable at the state level.

At a lower level of government, states, cities, and counties, or their agencies issue municipal bonds to fund an array of projects such as stadiums, sewers, utility services, schools, hospitals, and general budgetary needs. Municipal bonds are not as safe as those issued by the federal government. This is why you should always research the quality of any municipal bond through a rating service such as Moody's, Standard & Poor's, or Fitch.

In my disciplines the only acceptable category of risk for buying municipals is that they be AAA rated. Many municipalities purchase insurance on their bonds in order to receive a AAA rating. If municipalities do buy insurance on their bonds, I insist that the credit rating of the municipality which is issuing the bond to be at least an A grade. Another of my buy disciplines is to stay away from bonds subject to the Alternative Minimum Tax (AMT). Although the yields on AMT bonds are higher, investors face the increased risk that the bonds could become taxable at some point in time depending on the investor's circumstances. This is why I prefer to avoid them.

One other discipline I like to follow whenever possible is to buy bonds at par or at a discount. This means that you are paying the same amount, or less, than what the bonds will return at maturity. Some people will want you to buy bonds at a premium or more than what they will pay at maturity. Later I will describe this in more detail, but for the moment suffice it to say that the slightly higher yield for a premium bond is not worth the accounting!

Additionally I recommend that you buy and maintain a minimum of five positions in your account, all with staggered maturities. Your bonds should be owned outright, and unless being actively managed you should pay no annual fee on the account that you hold these bonds in. Such a fee would reduce your cash flow and is really not warranted. All my disciplines for buying bonds are based on the assumption you are buying and holding them to maturity with income and security as your primary goal.

You may be wondering what the advantages are for buying municipal bonds as opposed to other types. They tend to be more popular with people who are in the higher tax brackets and wish to reduce their tax burden. First of all the income stream from municipal bonds is not subject to federal income tax. They may also be sheltered from state and municipal taxes depending on where the bond was issued and where you, the bondholder, live. Municipal bonds should pay slightly less than comparable Treasury bonds so they don't make sense as an investment unless you need to shelter a certain portion of your investment from taxation.

Figuring out if municipal bonds are right for you requires you or your accountant do the proper calculations to compare municipals with the ultimate yield after tax from a portfolio that utilizes taxable bonds of the same yield, maturity, and quality with municipal bonds.

There is another consideration for owning municipal bonds that has nothing to do with taxation; that is quality. Historically municipal bonds have a very low rate of default, or non-payment. As such, they may be a better credit risk than owning some corporate bonds with a lower credit rating.

There are special trading techniques I use with bonds which are traditionally assets one buys and holds for a long period of time. However, part of my obligation to do the best for my clients is to have sell disciplines in place.

There are times when it is not to your advantage to hold municipal bonds to maturity. The most obvious signal to sell comes when your bond has been downgraded from its AAA rating. You also need to be wary when a bond's underlying rating is downgraded from that minimum "A" rating we insist upon. Remember that a municipal bond often achieves a AAA rating through insurance.

The underlying rating is the rating of the municipality itself. If the municipality's underlying rating is downgraded, it could be a sign of trouble and puts it into the sell category in my view. However, if the insurance companies have downgraded the bond, but the underlying credit of the insured bond is actually better, why sell? Sometimes what makes the difference in a buying or selling decision is the comparative opportunity cost of the money rather than any potential loss of principal. It may make sense to sell a bond if a much higher yield becomes available.

The message is that you can not simply buy bonds and forget them. I do credit checks on the bonds I buy several times a year. While bonds do not change their rating very often, you should maintain an awareness of their quality and any changes that might arise.

As I said, sometimes you can sell a bond to buy a better one. You might be in a position to capture an economically significant premium. You can sometimes buy a premium bond that has the same yield as a par bond. A premium bond has a higher coupon, and you will pay more for the maturity payoff than you will be repaid at maturity. The difference between what you pay for it and what it will mature for basically offsets the higher coupon. So you get the premium amount you paid for the bond in the form of a tax free coupon on a municipal bond. You get a little every year as the bond goes towards maturity.

You might perhaps pay $110 for a bond that matures at $100. The difference in these two figures is given back to you along the way in interest. In this example you might get a return of five percent instead of four percent. That one percent difference in interest equates with the ten percent difference in the price of the bond.

In general I am not a big fan of premium bonds because most investors have a difficult time with the concept. They usually do not understand why they are paying $110 for something that matures at $100. Even though they are getting that one percent back in the form of greater coupons every year, they have a hard time setting that money aside as principal rather than spendable income. As a result of this misunderstanding, many people unknowingly spend the whole coupon which contains a portion of their principal. The last thing I want my clients to do is spend their principal. The challenge of actually setting aside that small portion of principal from every coupon is an accounting headache to be sure!

There are also times you might want to sell in order to capture losses. Just as bonds can go up in price, they can go down in price. We know for sure that the price drop is temporary because bonds will mature at par value. There are points in time when bonds are trading at significant discounts to their maturity value. This happens more often when you have an environment of rising interest rates. Bonds will go down in price. At some point it makes sense to trade those bonds. It is called a bond swap. I might swap bonds that mature in five years for another set of bonds that mature in five years. This means you now have a sale, and with that sale comes a capital loss which can be used to offset other gains.

The good part is that you haven't really lost any of your principal because you will have the same amount of par value. You will also have the same amount of cash flow because you are trading equal yields. The downside is that you will lose a small amount of money to transaction costs. I never try to capture losses without making sure it makes economic sense to do the trade. If it does make sense, as part of your rebalancing you might want to harvest losses annually in order to offset any capital gains from other portions of your portfolio, or simply to have them to give you tax planning flexibility.

Most buyers of bonds are aware of credit risk and interest rate risk, but they tend to overlook the risk of inflation. You may be losing purchasing power every year. How much depends upon the inflation rate. Back in 1997 the federal government issued a new kind of Treasury bond to protect investors against the effects of inflation. This new type of bond is known as Treasury Inflation-Protection Securities, or TIPS.

While TIPS sound like a good hedge against inflation, I generally don't recommend buying them. Their rate of return is paltry. It generally runs a little over 1%. Granted, this is a real rate of return as the bond principal is increasing with inflation and this coupon is in addition to that inflation adjustment. The treasury does make adjustments for increases in the Consumer Price Index by adjusting the par value of the bond twice a year. But that creates another issue. Unless TIPS are held in a nontaxable account, the inflation-related appreciation you will get by purchasing TIPS will be taxed as well as the income from the bond.

If you elect to buy corporate bonds rather than bonds issued by the government, you will most likely receive a higher yield. But buyers of corporate bonds face a number of risks that are not normally associated with government backed securities.

The most important risk is default. You can guard against this by utilizing the same buy disciplines I adhere to when buying municipal bonds. However, with corporate bonds my ratings criteria are somewhat different. While a AAA rating is still desirable for all maturities, if you are buying a corporate bond with a maturity of less than five years, an A rating is acceptable. For maturities of less than ten years, your bond should carry at least a AA rating.

If your bonds are all AAA rated, then you need to hold only five positions. If they are AA rated, that number goes up to seven positions. And if you are purchasing A rated bonds, then you should raise the number to ten positions.

Another concern is the volatility of corporate bonds. During robust economic times the stock of the company which issued a particular bond may rise. As a result, the company's bonds would likely get a boost by credit rating agencies. This would push up the bonds' market value although your interest payments would remain the same. But the flip side is the danger of an economic downturn or sagging fortunes in the life of a particular company. If a company appears to be in trouble, the credit ratings on its bonds could be slashed and the market value of the bonds could plummet.

You should also take tax consequences into account if you are considering corporate bonds. They offer no protection against federal, state, or local taxes. Even if corporate bonds are held in a tax deferred account, the tax bill will eventually become due.

Many people who are afraid of the discipline of buying and laddering bonds, opt for bond funds instead. An investment in a bond fund is much like an investment in any other mutual fund. But there are drawbacks. A bond fund has no maturity date. There is no assurance that you will get every penny of your principal back even if the fund has invested solely in rock solid securities like Treasuries. It would be a big mistake to confuse a bond fund with an ordinary bond investment because it comes with no guarantees. It is also my personal observation that there are very few bond funds that can justify their fees in terms of extra performance.

There is a fairly new form of mutual fund geared towards retirement that is comprised of bonds as well as stocks. As investors approach age sixty-five, the mutual fund manager shifts the allocation of the fund almost exclusively to the most secure bonds, with little or no allocation to equities. But age sixty-five is way too early to go into capital preservation mode because life expectancy has increased greatly. If you are invested too heavily in bonds, the inflation I spoke about will erode your purchasing power.

Another problem is that many financial publications and websites offer you mathematical formulas to follow for asset allocation using your age as the determining factor. They usually say that your age is the percentage of your portfolio that should be invested in bonds. As an example, if you are sixty years old, then sixty percent of your assets should be in bonds. The fallacy is that your total asset pool is perceived as carrying less risk due to the amount that is invested in bonds. It is assumed that at older ages you do not have the ability to rebuild your assets. This is and has been the prevailing conventional wisdom for as long as I can remember.

But let's go back to the 1970s. If you were seventy years old and seventy percent in bonds, by the time you reached the age of eighty the purchasing power of your money would have declined by thirty percent. This was due to the high inflation that occurred in the second half of that decade alone. You would have found it almost impossible to meet even your most basic living expenses. But then as the 1980's unfolded, you would have found your income going down as interest rates declined. Your costs would have inflated and your income would be decreasing!

You must have adequate inflation protection to maintain your quality of life. The only answer is to create a customized diversified portfolio with my asset allocation model which will see you through all economic times.

SAVING FOR YOUR FUTURE

America has become a debtor nation, and this is disastrous on both a personal and macroeconomic level. For the first time in history we have a personal savings rate of minus 0.5%, and our national debt has soared into the trillions of dollars with no end in sight. Much of this debt is now held by foreign governments which puts our future position as the world's only true superpower in a great deal of jeopardy.

While as a nation we are in unchartered waters, as individuals we need to take personal responsibility for our debt and stop the bleeding. We need to turn that negative 0.5% savings rate into a positive 10%. We have to learn to say no to the combined insidious influences of Madison Avenue and the credit card companies. But saving even a small amount takes time, commitment, and discipline. The only way to do it is to start with a plan for what I refer to as "survival independence."

Survival freedom starts with creating not just one, but two budgets. The first budget should show what your basic needs are just to exist. Everything else goes into your "wants" budget. Many of the clients I see have a different concept of what they *think* is necessary versus what is really necessary.

At the end of this book you will find a fairly extensive annual budget. I suggest you go through each of the budget items and ask yourself what each item really means to you and if there are expenditures you can cut or lower. You should be able to articulate why each expenditure is a need rather than a want. When I do this with my own clients, I usually hear an amazing number of rationalizations and justifications.

As an example, a client of mine might be driving a giant gas-guzzling Ford 350. With fuel prices as high as they are, I want to know if the vehicle is being used for work or just for personal transportation. Unless it is a vital work tool, such an expensive machine is nothing more than a toy that a client may legitimately want and even enjoy but certainly does not *need*, especially if savings are important.

The issue of "needs" as opposed to "wants" frequently comes up during a discussion of a client's utility bills. In this day and age most people consider cable or satellite television a need. Cable and satellite companies are aware of this and often charge a king's ransom for premium services in addition to adding taxes that border on extortion. However, in reality most people who live in or near a town of any size can get a wealth of programming off the airwaves simply by using an antenna. Just making this one change can save the average household more than sixty dollars a month or over seven hundred dollars a year.

While my "needs" budget test may sound severe, I don't want to impose my own definition of what is absolutely necessary because this definition varies from client to client. What my exercise is intended to do is discover what is a client's minimum standard of life requires. Ultimately my goal is to show them the amount of cash flow that must be generated just for them to survive at a reasonable level. When they have accumulated the assets to generate this amount of cash flow, they have arrived at what I call survival independence.

As I have said, my clients' needs vary greatly. For instance, I advise a couple who insist that for their own emotional well being they absolutely need to go out to dinner on a "date night" once a week. No problem. My approach in this case was to build this expense into their needs budget and set aside enough money so they could go to their favorite spots, The Red Lobster and The Olive Garden. After a while, with a savings discipline and with the accumulation of assets, they were able to afford to dine out at more expensive restaurants like Morton's and The Palm. Fortunately they never lost the ability to keep their weekly date which was so important to their relationship.

When most people go through my budgeting process, they have no idea of what expenses are reasonable. Even though I normally eschew advice given by the media, I do respect the guidelines given by Jean Chatzky of *Money* magazine. According to her research, housing costs including mortgage payments, maintenance, repairs, taxes, and insurance should be no more than thirty percent of your budget. Transportation which includes car payments, gas, parking, insurance, repairs, and other transit may comprise eighteen percent. Food and toiletries are fourteen percent, and utilities should be seven percent. And I would personally add in a savings rate of ten percent or more.

Your percentages will be different I am sure, and these are just guidelines for you to consider At different times in your life, different categories will rise and fall in importance. For example, if you are older, then medical expenses will be a bigger part of your budget, and housing may be less as you may have purchased your home many years before.

Ideally my clients will realize that by constructing a "needs" budget they will be better off sacrificing a bit now in order to build an asset base so they can afford those things which will really add to their quality of life long term. Those are the items I have asked them to include in their "wants" budget.

As a financial advisor I don't want anybody to be forced to remain on a minimum survival budget. I want them to accumulate enough assets so they can live the rest of their lives at a sustainable, affordable, and enjoyable lifestyle.

If you can ascertain your survival budget and then try living on it as long as possible, you will continue to build principal, and things can only get better from there. Not only will you build assets, you will most likely find saving becomes second nature. At some point excessive spending won't be desirable to you as a way of life; it will feel unnecessarily and uncomfortably wasteful when you know you could be building up your future lifestyle by building your portfolio instead. I know a couple who failed to save anything for the future even though they had been successfully self-employed for over a decade. At one point they were able to maintain fairly lavish residences in Toronto, London, and Miami. Unfortunately most of their clients came from referrals, and the person who gave them the vast majority of their referrals retired to satisfy his political aspirations. On top of that, the association that governed their condominium in Miami levied a fifty thousand dollar assessment for structural repairs on all owners.

My clients learned about the concept of delayed gratification in a hurry. They got rid of two of their three residences. They sold one of their cars. Instead of going out for entertainment, they joined Netflix for five dollars a month. They allowed themselves to eat out only once a week and that was at McDonalds. And when they went to McDonalds, they ordered only off the dollar menu. The one luxury they allowed themselves was their gym membership because they could justify it for health reasons.

Fortunately they were not only able to survive that year without dipping into principal; they were even able to fund their Roth IRAs and start a retirement plan for their business. I am happy to say that soon after that difficult year they were able to find dependable employment but continue to live frugally out of habit, as if every dollar is their last.

During that difficult year the stock market was also down, but it didn't matter a great deal to my friends because they weren't using a penny of their principal. The volatility of their principal was not a pressing issue. They focused instead on the anticipated annual income on their monthly statements. And through the process of compounding, they found that their income statements only went up in value.

If you go back to your budget and run the equation backwards, the annual cash flow you need will dictate the assets you will need to generate that cash flow. Obviously the lower your spending, the lower the level of assets you need to put aside.

Working off a "needs" budget is far less daunting than working off a "wants" budget. A "wants" budget will cause you to feel that you will have to generate a huge pile of money for your future. I see people often become so daunted by their gigantic "wants" budget that they do the worst thing, nothing! They don't even start! My advice is to begin slowly, defining what is realistic for you to earn and save and then letting that nest egg compound and grow.

The question that follows is how much should you save? If you begin to save at a young enough age you can start by putting aside ten percent of everything you make. In addition to saving ten percent or more, you should also be saving half of the net raises you get during your working lifetime. This allows you to reward yourself for your advancement, but also to truly increase your savings without impacting your lifestyle negatively. Remember, the sooner you can build an asset base that will generate the income you need to live on, the sooner you will not *have* to work. At that point you can save 100% of what you are making from your job and build the asset base. As the asset base grows it generates more income and your lifestyle increases, but importantly never decreases! And if you continue this savings habit throughout your working life, you will probably acquire enough money to afford a very nice lifestyle in retirement. In fact it will most likely give you the same cash flow that you had in your peak earnings year adjusted for inflation.

But if you have waited and not started to accumulate any savings at all or if you have had severe reversals of fortune that were not of your own making, then the percentage of your gross income you will need to save increases substantially. The harsh reality is that if you have waited and not started saving until very late in your working career, then you will have a very difficult time accumulating enough of a financial asset pool to be able to sustain your lifestyle on the cash flow it generates. While you are working, you are the asset that generates the income you pay our expenses with. If you have not accumulated the assets to produce the income to pay for your lifestyle, then to maintain that lifestyle you will have to continue being an asset that generates cash flow by working beyond what most people consider their retirement age. This is why I say to save as much as you can as early as you can because you never know what is going to happen.

With the sophisticated financial planning software that is available to most advisors today, an analysis of where you stand toward achieving your financial independence can be done with relative ease. This software will take into account all of your assets, your projected benefits from social security, your life expectancy, your age and a host of other factors and assumptions to solve a complex algorithm to tell you how much you need to save every year to reach your goals. I have yet to meet anyone who came into my office that did not already know whether or not they were on track to achieve their goals. But a financial advisor can tell you how best to achieve them.

Many people who have not begun to accumulate financial assets have asked for some simple formula to know how much they need to save of their income each year to achieve financial independence. There are many different factors that go into answering that question. First, for how long will you be saving? Obviously the longer you can save and have the accumulated savings compound and grow, the smaller the percentage of your income that will need to be set aside each year. The answer to this question also has to do with how old are you now and at what age you wish to have enough financial independence so that your salary is no longer part of the equation generating the cash flow necessary to pay your expenses.

Second, what will your expenses be at that point in the future when you want to stop working? This is of course the most important factor in determining how large an asset base you will need to generate the income to cover those expenses. If your house will be fully paid for, the cars are all bought and paid for, money set aside for the kids' educations, you have no debt, and other large expenses are taken care of, then your expense budget may go down in retirement.

Third, what is your life expectancy and do you plan to leave an inheritance? Knowing the answer to this question tells us if the asset base itself can be utilized to meet some of those expenses and how long we need it to last. This is a perilous plan. Any time you start to spend the principal, you subject yourself to many risks outside your control and have no flexibility in responding to unanticipated events. It would not take too many years of significant inflation to devastate your asset base. The above are all questions, along with other considerations, that are unique to each person, but that need to be considered to come up with a realistic answer to your specific situation.

However, this is a common sense book and there is a common sense formula that you can use as a guide. It has just a few assumptions to it: first, that you are just starting to save and have no accumulated savings, second, that you will be investing your money as we have outlined in this book for the long term, third, that you will be disciplined in following the guidelines year after year, and fourth that you have at least 10 years to save.

This formula is to take whatever age you are now and subtract 10 from it. The resulting number is the percentage of your income that you will need to save every year between now and age 65.

So if you are 25 years old with no savings at all, you can save 15% of what you are making and fully expect that when you are 65 years old that you will be able to retire and have cash flow from your financial assets that will be equal to your peak earnings year. Co-incidentally that is the amount that you can elect to put into your 401(K) plan from a simple salary deduction.

However, if you are 40 years old, you would need to save 30% of what you are making for the next 25 years assuming you were starting with no savings at all. Obviously if you have some savings, a 401(K), an IRA, or some investments, the percentage would be a smaller number.

If you are 55 years old, then you would need to save 45% of what you are making now every year. Even with saving 45% a year, because of the shorter time frame there is a greater dependence on the investment results being predictable and consistent for those years of savings. This may seem daunting and undoable. However, most people after they turn 50 have already accumulated most of the "things" they need in their lives. They have the furniture, they have the cars, and they have a wardrobe (and, hopefully, will not outgrow it at this age!). Also, they probably have finished with some of the additional major expenses such as paying for college educations or helping with their parents' nursing home bills. Let us hope that they have been saving something in a retirement account so they are not starting from zero as well.

It is not a perfect formula, and it does not take into account far too many variables that can affect the outcome. These are things like the rate of salary increases, year to year investment returns, inflation rates, bonuses, and any other one time lump sums that might be added such as inheritances.

One of the biggest assumptions in this formula is an increasing salary over the years. It assumes a 5% increase on an annual basis. While you may not get that extra five percent each and every year, I am sure that if you were to look back over the last twenty years of your career, you would see that you averaged a raise of five percent annually. And while 5% in any one year does not seem like a lot, in 14.4 years it will double your salary.

If you see this is not happening as time goes on, a red flag should go up signaling that perhaps you should be more proactive regarding compensation for all your hard work. While it might seem drastic, you may even look at the benefit of switching employers. But the other reason you might see a red flag may be your fault. It means you must substantially increase your savings rate or you will be in big trouble when it comes time to retire.

Another large assumption in my formula is the rate of return on the investments you are accumulating. I have factored in the asset allocation disciplines of this book, and using a back testing of my methods of investing for over 30 years, I have used a return assumption of 10.5%. There is no guarantee that past performance can be duplicated in the future. And if it is not achieved, then obviously either more savings or more time will be needed to accumulate the assets needed to generate the cash flow for your financial independence. In order to avoid delaying the date of your financial independence, when you can work because you want to and not because you have to, you should consider trying to implement this formula: At forty years old you should be saving thirty percent of your salary. At fifty years old your savings ought to rise to forty percent. The good news is that most people are not in this kind of bind because they are not starting from zero. They usually have put at least some money away in a 401(K) or an IRA.

Most financial pundits will tell you to get out of debt first before you even think about saving. But I believe if you take this advice, you will have lost out on the discipline of saving and compounding. I would suggest instead that you put only half the money you have put aside to reduce your debt load and use the other half to begin your savings program. Even if you are stuck with high credit card debt, in the long run it is absolutely critical for you to accumulate assets. Of course you should pay off the debt with the highest interest rates first and then use every mechanism available to lower your debt and reduce the interest you may be paying on that debt.

You can start first by calling your credit card companies. You may be surprised by how willing they are to work with you if you threaten to take your business elsewhere. They may give you a much lower rate if you agree to implement a repayment plan. Show them how seriously you take your situation. They will be highly motivated to come to a mutually advantageous agreement if they know you will actually pay off your debt and still pay them some degree of interest at the same time. The key is to take action the minute you get into trouble (preferably before you have trouble). Otherwise you will have a much harder time establishing your credibility. This is the same method that many of the credit consolidating companies use, but why should you pay extra for a middleman to intervene when you can do this yourself?

Another way to lower your credit card payments is to start opening your junk mail. You are no doubt being besieged on a daily basis by credit card companies offering a low teaser interest rate. If you take advantage of these offers only as long as the low rates apply, you will be able to lower your monthly payments. I do have to give you one word of caution here. These cards are deliberately designed to be misleading so make sure you understand every detail of the companies' terms before implementing this strategy. And be very cautious of any "transfer fees". Again, if you call the companies these fees may be waived so that they can obtain your business.

By the way, I am not telling you to cut up all your credit cards because you need to keep one card in case of a real emergency. However, don't carry that card around with you as you stroll through the mall or go out to dinner. You will be amazed at how your definition of what constitutes an emergency can change. Instead keep your one credit card in a special place that requires you to go through a series of several steps to get at it. This will give you more time to think whether you are spending your money on a true emergency or not.

You might be tempted to hand your emergency card over to your spouse or a trusted friend. But it is unfair to put someone else in the position of being your banker. It is also unwise because of the likelihood that you may damage your relationship if you disagree over the use of the card. Perhaps the best solution to the problem is to keep a debit card instead of a credit card for emergencies. If you do decide to keep a credit card instead, I suggest keeping the one that also provides you with overdraft protection on your checking account so you will never have to pay outrageous bank fees for a bounced check. Remember to check on the fees associated with using a debit card! Many banks will reimburse these charges in order to attract your business.

Many financial pundits suggest you actually set aside a fund for critical unforeseen expenses. Whether or not that is necessary and how much one puts into the fund is up to the individual. The rule of thumb used to be that you should put aside enough to cover living expenses for three months. That number has increased to six months as economic uncertainty has increased in the United States. Deciding how much to put in reserve, depends partly on the liquidity of the assets. I would suggest that the older you are, the more prudent it is to create a larger fallback position.

The average sixty year-old who loses his job today, usually takes at least ten months to find new employment. Unfortunately, studies show that job will pay only an average of sixty percent of his current income. The figures are even worse for mature women.

There is another even more frightening statistic; if you remain unemployed for a period of a year or more, the chances are ninety percent you will never go back to work full time. This is another reason I put such an emphasis on saving early while you are in a position to do so.

If you happen to lose your job or suffer another kind of financial reversal, it is critical that you go into financial survival mode immediately. If you do this without delay, you might find that three months of income may cover your expenses for six months but only if you severely tighten your belt.

If you have set up your suggested emergency fund in advance, the key is to place it in a segregated account that you should never look at or use it unless you encounter a true emergency. There are now several reliable Internet banks that are insured by the FDIC. They usually pay a better rate of return than you would get elsewhere on either a savings or money market account. These can be linked to your personal home bank accounts so that free wire transfers can be accomplished within twenty-four hours.

I suggest you consider using one of these Internet banks for a very practical reason. If you keep your emergency reserve money in your checking account, you may begin to feel the money is spendable. In order to avoid that temptation it is prudent to keep as little in your checking account as is practical.

If you also have your extra cash in a brokerage account that either automatically issues you a related credit card or gives you blank checks, get rid of them. Over my years as a wealth manager it is astounding how often I have seen a client's perceived need for something overcome their prudent financial stewardship. It is difficult to watch the assets I have worked so hard to help them obtain go down the drain. There is a saying which I find to be very true, "Emergencies know how much is in your checkbook."

So far we have talked about saving for people who receive a predictable and dependable salary while they are working. But there are also certain industries where money is not made in an ongoing fashion but in chunks which are earned periodically. This is true of the entertainment industry, sports, some writers, architects, interior designers, builders, landscapers, and many types of artists. Another way in which unpredictable money comes in is from bonuses for those who work in sales. In fact, whole industries are becoming commission driven in lieu of dependable salaries. This method of compensation can place the whole onus of survival, not to mention savings, on you, the earner.

There can be very long intervals between cash payments, and the amount may vary greatly. If this describes your situation, you should not live according to your income when you receive it. I have stories of two friends who did not obey this advice and learned to regret it.

I remember a twenty-seven year old salesman who was making forty thousand dollars a year and living very comfortably on that. One day he landed a very large account, and as a result, his income doubled. He immediately took on the lifestyle of someone who was making eighty thousand a year. The problem was he had gotten the big account by taking it away from a fellow salesman. Warning bells should have gone off that this new client did not prize loyalty. I'm sure you can guess what happened next. He lost the account the following year to yet another salesman so his annual income plummeted back down to forty thousand.

But the bad situation did not end there. Because my friend had spent so much time servicing his important new client, he had let his old accounts lapse even though they had always been his bread and butter. Ultimately he found himself bringing in less than thirty-five thousand a year. He decided to dip into his savings to keep his eighty thousand dollar lifestyle going. Within a year he had absolutely nothing in the bank.

The real tragedy of this outcome is that it was so unnecessary because the salesman, who had no dependents, had been perfectly happy living on a budget of forty thousand. If he had only saved the extra forty thousand from his new client, ultimately he would have been far closer to being set for life. Apparently he is not alone in his spending folly. Almost two thirds of all lottery winners go bankrupt within the space of two years. The moral of this story is that if you are in a sales position and can live off your salary, invest all the bonuses you get into your portfolio.

If you are in a profession like those I mentioned which pay sporadically, you are in a potentially precarious situation and must mitigate against the dangers by building up your cash reserves as fast as possible. You should pay particular attention to the expense side of your cash flow equation. This is particularly important because workers who do not receive an ongoing paycheck are usually the ones who must also get along without company benefits such as health insurance which are so important in times of crisis.

I can give you a real life illustration of this with another example. Another gentleman I know was widely regarded as a dashing and a brilliant, award-winning novelist. His specialty was mysteries based on historical figures. By the time he was in his fifties he had published seven books in America and at least ten in Germany and France.

His fame caused him to feel financially entitled to buy a home in the Greek islands, one in Santa Fe, and one in Los Angeles. At every large dinner party with his large circle of adoring fans, he picked up the tab. Then he began to collect vintage motorcycles which he paid several thousand dollars to transport to wherever he was living.

But his sales figures were declining with each successive book, and publishers began to take note. During the course of his writing career the publishing industry had changed. In order to secure a contract with his early books all he had to do was submit an outline and a sample first chapter. But now his literary agent will not pass anything along to a publisher unless it is a completed manuscript (which usually takes him at least a year to write). My friend has not published a book in the United States in over ten years.

Reluctantly he was forced to go back to his college job of bartending. The stress of this hardship was so great that he started drinking to excess until he found himself in the emergency room of a major medical center. By the time he emerged, he had over two hundred thousand dollars in medical bills and no health insurance. Fortunately he was able to get himself classified as a charity case, and he has not taken another drink.

Today he is a broken man who puts a roof over his head by house-sitting the homes of his former wealthy friends. If he had only saved half the royalties from his novels, he most likely could have avoided a painful downward spiral that still has no end in sight.

It is so tempting in this culture of conspicuous consumption to live well beyond your means. It has now become the American way of life. But there was a study conducted in 2007 that revealed the correlation between an individual's happiness and their degree of wealth. The research showed that a person's maximum happiness required an income of roughly fifty thousand dollars. But no matter how much they earn above that level, they find no greater sense of satisfaction with life. In fact many become less happy because as they pursue the so-called American dream of greater and greater wealth and the toys it buys, the amount of extra work required often puts a strain on family relationships.

If you want to pursue that dream, then you would be far better off viewing it from a different perspective. Instead of seeing the goal as the acquisition of goods, look at it as the acquisition of *income-producing assets*. What you are ultimately buying is peace of mind. Peace comes from the knowledge that no matter how long you live, you will always have enough money to sustain yourself and your spouse. That is a gift to yourself that is absolutely priceless.

CHOOSING A FINANCIAL ADVISOR

A good financial advisor will help you review and understand all the fundamentals you need as an investor. The key is to find someone you can work with over a long period of time in a relationship that is in many ways as intimate as the relationship you have with your family doctor. But before considering hiring a financial advisor, you need to figure out several things.

If you already have a financial advisor, why do you want to make a change? The most common reason clients give for changing is a lack of contact from the person who is managing their money. If you are unhappy in this or any other regard, you should at least address the problem first with your current advisor. Sometimes difficulties are merely a result of miscommunication. You may feel that you require quarterly meetings while the advisor may assume you do not wish to be disturbed unless it is absolutely necessary. You owe it to yourself and to the person who has helped you with your investing to at least talk things over.

Sometimes the partnership simply will no longer work. There may be a tangible reason for this. It is certainly not unheard of for a successful advisor to go through his list of clients and divide them into A, B, and C categories He may decide to concentrate only on his A list clients because they are the ones who bring him the most revenue. This means he may be perfectly content to lose his C list clients through attrition by failing to service them properly. You will most likely know where you stand by seeing how hard your advisor tries to keep you. If he makes little or no effort, it is probably time to look elsewhere for an advisor who cares a lot more about your finances.

If you are a person who has always done his own investing, you may wonder about the actual need for consulting a professional. Certainly there is a lot of financial information out there on the Internet and in a vast array of magazines and specialized newspapers. But Kevin Keller, CEO of the Certified Financial Planner Board of Standards, contends that it is the advisor's role to translate all that information into actionable knowledge for his clients.

And while you might be able to get by without seeking counsel, having a good advisor is like having a good personal trainer. You might know that you need to do thirty minutes of aerobic exercise a day to keep your heart in good health, but the question is will you do it on your own or would you do it more regularly and more effectively with a coach?

You also have to ask yourself if you truly have the experience and training to put together the proper investment plan that will ensure you reach your goals in the necessary time frame. There are many variables and permutations which are part of financial decisions that you may not be aware of as a lay person.

The other difficulty is remaining perfectly calm and detached during volatile times. We know that many investment decisions are emotionally driven. Hiring a professional takes the emotionality out of your decision-making process regarding all aspects of your investment plan. In order to have the best of both worlds, independence *and* professional experience, having a totally objective financial advisor who at least reviews your decisions in what is known as a "self-directed account" might well be a good compromise.

Whether or not you need a particular advisor's outside help may be a function of what is known as "alpha." Alpha is the incremental rate of return added by a portfolio manager and their securities selection or asset allocation decisions over and above an index. As an example, you can on your own go out and buy an investment which tracks the Dow Jones Industrial Average Index through a number of different investment vehicles. However, let's say your portfolio manager decided to buy only twenty-nine of the thirty Dow Jones stocks because he felt the thirtieth was going to be a loser. The difference between performance of his twenty-nine picks and the Dow Jones would be the alpha. It can be either a positive or negative number. A positive number and the advisor is adding value to the investment account more than just buying the index. A negative number and you would have been better off in the index. This of course assumes that the index was the right investment for you and your risk tolerance. We would not want to compare your accounts performance to that of an index which was not indicative of your personalized portfolio.

Just how do you go about finding that perfect advisor? You should always conduct your search through personal interviews. But sometimes it is difficult to find out exactly whom to interview. With other types of professional services, people often ask their friends for a referral. However, when it comes to financial advice friends are often hesitant. While they may happily give you the name of their dentist, or dermatologist, talking about one's personal money is still a big taboo.

Because the best source for any professional is satisfied clients, I would strongly suggest you disregard that taboo and query your friends and associates for the names of financial advisors who have met or exceeded their expectations. Make it clear you are not asking them to divulge any of their information, just the name of whom they feel comfortable working with. If possible, I would suggest you try to get referrals from those friends who appear to be in roughly the same economic category as yourself.

It is helpful to find out if your assets are in the range the advisor usually works with. If he advises clients with assets of a million dollars or more, and you come in with three hundred thousand, you may find your portfolio overlooked, or you may find yourself shunted off to one of the junior members of the team.

Another way to find a good advisor is to go to the branch managers of several brokerage houses and tell them what you are seeking. Ask the branch manager to assign someone to you who meets your needs. This puts a large ethical and legal onus on the branch manager to match you with the appropriate advisor. Just make sure you make it clear are not to be placed with the person on staff who is in the greatest need of acquiring new accounts.

Another way to garner names is through a professional referral, but this is becoming less common. A few years ago you could ask your family attorney or accountant whom he would recommend. However, with the volatility of the financial markets being what it has been many attorneys and accountants have seen their clients lose money, and they do not want to jeopardize their client relationships so they have become much more reluctant to give recommendations. They simply do not want the liability or ill will that could result if their client should face a financial reversal as a result of their referral. Another difficulty is that these professionals are constantly besieged by advisors to give their names as recommendations. Rather than showing favoritism, they simply make it a policy not to refer anybody to anyone.

Accountants are sometimes in a special situation because increasingly many of them are also advertising themselves as financial advisors. The last thing they want to do is send you to a competitor. Since they routinely prepare your taxes, they usually are aware of all your assets. The next step for some accountants is to change their relationship with you so they perform a dual role as both an advisor and an accountant. What accountants often offer is an emphasis on tax-based financial planning advice. If taxes are a major problem for you, this may be to your advantage. Just make sure that the person you choose is as adept at investing as they are at accounting. Few can master both disciplines effectively. In my opinion, it is best to have the attorney, the accountant and the financial advisor work together in a collaborative process to help you achieve your financial independence. Each brings his unique expertise to the team.

Most advisors will give you a complimentary initial consultation. But before you take them up on this offer, you need to do a great deal of homework. First of all you need to develop a budget if you don't already have one. Without an understanding of your needs for income and growth from your investments it is difficult for an advisor to make a proper investment allocation recommendation. If you need help in coming up with a budget, there is a template you can use at the end of this book.

The second thing the broker will require is a complete list of your assets so he can determine how well you are already positioned. It is essential for the advisor to see all of the assets that you have, even if he or she will not be controlling those assets. Without a complete picture the advisor will not be able to make a proper recommendation. Once again a sample asset questionnaire of the type frequently used by financial advisors is included at the end of this book. While you probably don't have assets in all of the classes listed, you can use it as a guideline.

Generally when you go in for a first meeting with a financial advisor you will be asked to bring in your budget, a list of all your assets, and usually last year's tax return. Some brokers do not require this homework and prefer to gain this information simply through a series of questions. In either case you will find the appointment more rewarding if you have the as much personal financial information as possible on hand when you begin your interview.

Before you go to see a financial advisor, you should take the time to determine exactly what you want from him. Are you trying to get out of debt? If so, you might not need an advisor; you might need a credit counselor instead. Are you planning for your retirement? Then when are you planning to retire? What do you want your retirement to look like? Figure out what is important to you. The first step is defining your goals or you may wind up being susceptible to a sales pitch from an advisor who may be more intent on building his client list than helping you build your future.

The first meeting should be something like a first date. It is a time for both sides to get to know each other and see if they feel comfortable enough with each other to proceed together. Remember that this is just the initial step in what is, hopefully, a mutually rewarding relationship that will last for years. You want to work with a person who is willing to develop a plan for you over time and not push you into investments before you are ready.

You should expect to be asked questions about your tolerance for risk because you need to wind up with an investment plan that matches your personal risk profile, or what might better be referred to as your liquidity needs, as well as your goals and tolerance for volatility. Obviously if you are a person who is highly risk averse, you do not want to go to an options trader or a commodities broker for advice. You want someone who has demonstrated strengths in the areas you wish to focus on.

As someone who believes in helping clients create an overall financial plan and asset allocation model, I interview all my prospective clients extensively to determine their risk tolerance. Having been through many market cycles and experienced firsthand what risk really is about, I have learned over the years that often what someone tells you would be an acceptable level of risk, does not turn out to be true when they actually experience a decline in the value of an asset. That is why education and disciplines that people understand can provide the reassurance they need to weather difficult times. It also tends to lead to more conservative investment recommendations than the client initially thought they wanted. I find that most clients like the idea of higher returns until they are faced with the risk required to achieve them. Therefore I tend to urge a conservative approach in order to give my clients piece of mind. Otherwise I have not done my job.

Here I would like to offer a word of caution. Do not be fooled by a list of designations behind a person's name such as Certified Senior Specialist or Wealth Manager because many of these titles are utterly meaningless. Some of them are the results of the advisor attending very short seminars that will then provide them with a marketing-based title. What you are most likely looking for anyway is someone to be your "core advisor." This is the professional who acts as quarterback during the creation of your overall financial plan and helps you set the timelines and coordinate any other professionals you have on your team.

If you already have an estate attorney, an accountant, and an insurance specialist, ask if the prospective core advisor is willing to work with your team and act as the quarterback. If you don't already have a professional team in place, find out if your core advisor has a team of professionals he regularly works with so you can, if needed, create a truly comprehensive financial plan. Also, if you have a particular type of investment in mind that is somewhat outside the norm, find out if your core advisor has access to the "specialty advisors" you may require.

At your first meeting ask the advisor about his training, investment approach, and range of services. While it is too soon to ask for specifics, he should be able to give you broad advice about budgeting, saving, investments, taxes, and retirement planning.

If you are a couple, during the first appointment notice if the broker talks with both of you equally. Often much of the discussion with a prospective advisor occurs between the broker and the husband, leaving the wife all but completely ignored. This approach will surely lead to problems on down the line because both halves of a couple should be in complete agreement about whom they wish to hire. Remember you are creating a financial plan that covers the needs of both parties. Finance is one area that can cause stress at home. If both husband and wife are completely involved in the process then it can be a great stress reducer in the house.

Another factor in your decision should be how the broker gets paid. There are two ways you can pay for advice. One is on a transactional basis where you pay for each individual transaction such as a stock trade. Because the industry has become so commoditized, most people have forgotten that a part of the transactional fee or commission is intended to pay for the advisors' advice and counsel. If you elect this method, it is important to remember you are paying for the time, deliberation and experience that have gone into the decision-making process, and you are paying for a lot of help that is beyond the scope of a single transaction.

Over the last couple of decades another way of paying your advisor has become more popular. Compensation is based on a percentage the assets he or she is managing for you. This is often referred to as a wrap fee which a client typically pays the advisor on an annual basis and is billed quarterly. The advantage of this method is that there is a common bond between the client and the advisor because they both want the client's assets to continue to grow as quickly as possible for their mutual benefit. If the assets grow, the advisor gets paid more. And if the assets go down, the advisor gets paid less.

Both of these arrangements have their benefits and shortcomings so you need to know what is appropriate for you. However, your decision should be made on more than a simple dollars and cents basis. One of the potential downfalls of a wrap account is that the broker receives relatively stable income from your funds and may no longer be motivated to do as many transactions and fails to be as diligent as necessary.

On the other hand, a transactional broker receives no compensation unless there are transactions and, therefore, there is a potential conflict of interest. You should always know the economic reasons for any transaction. This may be the reason that most advisory fees (fifty-one percent) are paid by a combination of fees and commissions while only thirty-four percent are paid by fees alone. Certainly before signing with anyone you need to be completely aware of how the person is giving you advice is being compensated, and you should be completely comfortable with it.

Is the size of the advisor's organization important to you? Some clients feel more secure putting their money with a large established national firm. Others fear that at such a firm they will become lost in the shuffle or will be subject to mandates from the corporation that are passed down to the investment advisors. What fees does the firm charge, and do they have a minimum account size in order for you to work with one of their advisors? You should also find out what resources the firm has and whether the broker alone is responsible for delivering those resources to you. Will you continue to meet with the person who is conducting the first appointment or will you ultimately be assigned to work with another advisor? How often will your advisor review your investment plan with you, and will he do so in person? In other words, is he set up and prepared to meet your needs?

If you decide to go with a smaller one person firm, you will want to know what your advisor's plan of action will be in the event he or she becomes incapacitated. Or if the advisor appears to be nearing retirement, you should ask if there is a succession plan in place. While these questions may seem premature, remember that you are forging a relationship that could well last for twenty years or more and, hopefully, to the next generation!

Many times when you call your ,advisor, you will first have to speak to his staff who often act as gatekeepers. This is commonplace and should not be looked at negatively. These staff people many times are the very people you want to communicate with on a day to day basis to get service on your account. When investment questions or planning issues arise, the advisor will be the one with whom to talk. But for checks, address changes, requests for documents, making deposits or withdrawals the staff is there to help you. Make sure you are comfortable with those members of the staff as well as the advisor. You need to feel they will treat you and your concerns seriously and be empowered enough to take care of your questions when the advisor is not available.

If the advisor has met all of your concerns and you feel comfortable with him, you should agree to a second meeting. Usually there is still no charge. Before agreeing to the second appointment, however, you should always find out if there is any cost involved. If so, you should also find out exactly what you will be getting for your money. Sometimes advisors demand a fee as a test of the client's intentions in a second appointment. They want to know if it is worth their time to go through the trouble of creating a customized plan for a prospective client or if you are just window-shopping for free advice.

You most likely will do most of the talking during the first appointment so that you can explain what is important to you about your financial future. During the second appointment the roles are generally reversed. This is the time for the advisor to lay out for you the manner in which he intends to help you reach your goals.

Your goals will probably fall into one of five categories: income (cash flow and preservation of capital), income and growth (income and keeping up with inflation), growth and income (cash flow and growth), growth (capital appreciation and reinvestment of cash flow), and strategic equities (maximum long term growth). No matter what the category, you are looking for someone who knows how to provide you with the asset allocation that will deliver diversified, disciplined, long term investment solutions.

 Unfortunately many clients tend to associate their stockbroker or financial advisor with a certain class of investments. They may divide where they place their assets accordingly. In my case I deal with stocks, bonds, and real estate and I need to know *all* about a client's assets. A problem could arise if I don't have all the information because I construct my asset allocation model based on the money my clients have with me. If there are other assets I am not aware of, either with another adviser or investments which the client controls himself, I will be unable to do a proper job of asset allocation without being fully informed.

That's why I cannot express enough how important it is for you to be completely honest with your prospective broker about all the assets you hold and exactly how much cash flow you will require. You should also let him know whether or not you are planning on entrusting all of your assets to his care. If not, how will the assets he does not control be invested and what percentage of your net worth will that represent? And it is very important to decide what cash reserves you will maintain away from his control.

If you are not looking for a core advisor but for a specialty advisor, or someone to manage a more highly speculative small portion of your portfolio, you might be better served by not revealing the rest of your assets. Instead let your core advisor be the coordinator who knows all and sees all. And if you are the type of person we have discussed who wants a core advisor while still maintaining investment control over a portion of your assets in a self-directed account, you should at least ask your core advisor to give you the name of some investments which will complement the rest of your holdings.

If you don't like the advisor or their advice, you are under no obligation to return for another appointment. Believe me, they have had past rejections. Honestly, it is very unfair to take up an advisor's time with several appointments if you have no real intention of signing up with them.

Here's another potential hurdle. If you are impressed with a prospective advisor but uncomfortable dismissing your current advisor, you should ask yourself this question: "Am I in the relationship with my current advisor out of friendship or is it business?" While you know the answer should be purely business, probably over time it has become a bit of both. But it would be unwise to remain with an advisor who has delivered substandard returns simply because you like them.

Don't allow friendship to interfere with your financial future. Fortunately, you can change advisors without having to go through a personal confrontation. All you will have to do is sign a form that will authorize your former brokerage firm to transfer your assets to the new firm. This process is surprisingly simple and generally takes less than two weeks. Of course the courtesy of a note to the prior broker letting him know you are transferring the accounts can serve a dual purpose. In that note you can request a copy of all the documents that are in your client file for your records.

My advice is that once the assets are transferred, do not make any major investment decisions until you and your new advisor have completed the entire process of building your plan and understanding it.

Finally, I do have one important word of caution. Always look up the name of your potential new broker on the Financial Industry Regulatory or FINRA website to see if any actions have been filed or taken against him. FINRA was established in 2007 as a result of consolidation between the regulatory arm of the NASD and the New York Stock Exchange. It covers nearly five thousand brokerage firms, about 173,000 branch offices, and 676,000 registered securities representatives. FINRA also has a toll free number called the Brokercheck Hotline to help you check up on your prospective advisor's background. The number is 1-800-289-9999. Keep in mind though that anybody can write a letter of complaint. It is the final disposition of the complaint that matters.

Although problems are rare, I do know of a couple who was about to sign with a specialist in laddering bonds for one of the largest and most respected brokerage firms in America. Fortunately the husband did a background check and found that the person they were about to hire had been forced to pay an $800,000 fine levied by FINRA for misrepresentation. Needles to say, they were happy they performed their own due diligence.

When it comes down to it, my number one rule for selecting a financial advisor is to select someone who recognizes he is dealing with YOUR money. But because it is your money, it is also your responsibility to monitor how it is being managed. You should insist on such things as periodic reviews and rebalancing of your portfolio as well as showing a commitment to helping you achieve your necessary cash flow. In order to do so, you need to insist on full disclosure and transparency.

Quite simply, you need to choose someone you feel will always do the right thing for you no matter what the circumstances. If you find such a person, you will have created an invaluable relationship that could enrich the rest of your life.

HISTORICAL PERSPECTIVE ON INVESTING

For decades, indeed centuries, immigrants have been flooding across our borders both legally and illegally for the greatest prize of all, The American Dream. Whether they come from a third world country such as Ghana or from a country which some regard as a more sophisticated society than our own such as Britain, they know America is a unique and very special place. It is a place with an economy and social conscience that allows those with nothing to actually become part of the elite. Through education, hard work, and passion you can make a fortune from nothing in America.

Many societies have had periods of time when there is upwards mobility for most of the social classes. But no example is as striking as the United States. Here people can move from the lower class to the middle class and from the middle class to the upper middle class, and even a small percentage become billionaires. Even more impressive is the fact that in America citizens can attain a complete change in status in less than a generation. At its best, America is a true meritocracy.

But what truly defines America is that, more than any other country in the world, we have had a greater percentage of our population in the middle class. Of course, we have always also had the poor alongside the middle class and the rich, but here we have allowed the poor to dream. And here they can have at least some expectation that they can at least reach the next rung on the social and economic ladder.

What frightens me is that I see the middle class shrinking as a percentage of our population. The gulf between the "haves" and the "have-nots" is getting greater. As a student of history, I have seen that when the gulf becomes so wide that the "have-nots" no longer have a reasonable expectation of being able to progress to the next level, that society is ripe for revolution.

There is a dangerous tipping point when the wealth of the society is highly concentrated among those few who have assets. At the other end of the scale you have the great mass of the lower class, which poses a threat merely because of its sheer numbers. Of course, this situation exists all around the globe. But the difference in America is one of great expectations. And expectations tend to embolden, sometimes even leading to a change in the political structure.

Although it is almost never discussed, we have already had three economic revolutions in our country which have led to substantial political change. The first of these was in fact called "The Revolutionary War." The very fact that the hallmark quotation of this war was, "No taxation without representation!" demonstrates that we were the "have-not" colonies in opposition to the British aristocracy. This situation created a degree of social inequality that could not survive. Obviously this war was the genesis of the formation of what came to be known as the United States, but at the time it was not without internal controversy.

Each individual had to decide whether to become a patriot or remain a loyalist. This choice caused not only the first schism in the populace, but impacted American economic institutions both positively and negatively during the course of the war. For a time economic disorder reigned due to blockaded ports, routine shortages of necessary items, hyperinflation, and an increasingly worthless currency. However, because of the war, the colonies also gained revitalized community trade and exchange networks independent of Britain. In order to do so, the patriots enforced market controls and regulated prices of essential items as well as forbidding the exportation of locally needed foodstuffs.

Ultimately most wounds were healed as we gained our economic independence through open political revolution. As a result, we then adopted a society and government that allowed for equal rights. All people also had the right to be rich or poor depending upon not upon their station at birth but upon their own merit.

Our country began to grow and prosper and with it its people. As decades passed, unfortunately a deep divide started to emerge between the industrialized North and the agrarian South. We began to experience economic inequality again. Not only was there an economic divide, but also a divide in the social consciousness among Americans.

The system of slavery in the South absolutely prohibited their upward mobility. This was in stark contrast to the North which had the correct model of opportunity through upward mobility for all people. During the early 1900s historians even looked back upon what we now know as the Civil War, and some called it The Second American Revolution.

As everyone knows, it took the Civil War to decide which economic and social model was going to triumph. One could say that the better economic model won because the North was able to manufacture the armaments better and faster until it wore the South down. In fact because the South could not provide adequate wartime provisions, it may have lost the war as much economically as it did militarily.

Surprisingly statistical information suggests that the war exercised no major positive influence on Northern industry or may have actually retarded its growth (mainly due to inflation). But whether the Civil War was an impetus to industry or not, the North was clearly in the economic lead. At the beginning of the Civil War, the United States possessed some 128,300 industrial establishments. Of these, 110,274 were located in states that remained in the Union. Furthermore, the North contributed 92.5% of the $1.9 billion that comprised the gross national product in 1860. Looked at from an economic vantage point, during the Civil War the South simply didn't stand a chance.

The long term economic effects of the Civil War were fairly minor. Certainly the war years stimulated the production of some new inventions and accelerated the growth of some established technologies. But in reality the war gave rise to no new important industries and generated no unusual increase in basic industrial production. Also it did not, as some economists later asserted, spawn the American industrial revolution. Most of the innovations which did revolutionize American industry later in the nineteenth century had already been invented in the half century prior to the Civil War.

Perhaps the greatest effect of the wartime years was to prepare America for the intense industrialization that followed 1865. The stifling government restrictions that had existed in the United States prior to the Civil War were eliminated. The regional market system of the antebellum years was replaced by a national one. But most importantly political power fell into the hands of those who favored intense business growth.

The third economic revolution in this country was, like the Civil War, an internal one. It was caused by the Great Depression, a period of a few "haves" and a great preponderance of "have-nots." The Great Depression began when the market peaked in October of 1929. It was a time of full employment, but it was also a time of high leverage, or borrowing, which people should not have been using, and a dollar that was backed by gold. And when things began to unravel, they unraveled very quickly. Still America did not feel the depths of the Depression until several years later. The ultimate result of the Great Depression is that we went from a free enterprise system to a modified socialized system originally instituted as "The New Deal."

The New Deal was the title that President Franklin Roosevelt gave to a series of programs he initiated between 1933 and 1938. It was designed to give relief to the poor (or the "have-nots"), reform our financial system, and ensure America's recovery from The Great Depression. It was based on the now debunked belief that the federal government could solve all our financial problems. The New Deal of 1933 was first aimed at simple short term recovery programs for all parts of our society. It consisted of banking reform laws, emergency relief, regulatory oversight, and work relief programs.

The second New Deal, which came in 1935 and 1936, was a much more comprehensive redistribution of power and the nation's resources. It included union protection programs, the Social Security Act, and aid to tenant farmers and migrant workers. However, the Supreme Court ruled several of the New Deal programs unconstitutional. Others are still an important part of the economic and social fabric of America today.

Of course we all know that the Social Security System remains changed, but still intact. Along with it The New Deal created the Federal Deposit Insurance Corporation, the Federal Housing Administration, The Tennessee Valley Authority, Fannie Mae, and the Securities and Exchange Commission.

Quite simply the United States has greatly changed its society. We did not have welfare before the advent of this new system. Also the Federal Reserve, which had been manacled by a currency tied to actual reserves of gold, now, has as much power as it currently does to inject liquidity into our banking system.

No one had even thought of the concept of Medicare or Medicaid. We have truly revolutionized our society. Most importantly we did so without bloodshed.

Unfortunately with the increased financial disparity that I see on the rise in our country, much of it a natural result of several generations of the explosion of welfare and the "entitled" sub class of our society, I fear that our children will see another revolution. I can only hope it will once again be a bloodless one.

The problem we face is greater than the divide between the rich and poor. We have learned that many of our once sacrosanct financial institutions have become riddled with greed and corruption and must now be bailed out by the federal government. Furthermore, we must find the new renewable energy resources to allow us to continue to compete on a global scale.

We must find the diplomatic means to resolve international conflicts instead of funding armies around the world. We must support enough research to stave off pandemics which could decimate our population. We must become part of the solution to global warming or the very land we stand on will be forever changed. In fact, the challenges America faces are greater now than at any time in its past. We have no choice but to rise to the occasion. We have in the past, and I have every confidence we will now as well. But in my mind change will come again from the fundamental roots that have made our country great, a free and open society that allows those who work hard to succeed and prosper.

RIDING OUT A SYSTEMIC FINANCIAL CRISIS

There are rare but frightening periods in the evolution of our economy when all investment rules seem to go out the window, and the average investor does not know where to turn. Even though you have followed all the disciplines in this book, you may still find yourself beset by panic. The autumn of 2008 seemed like such a difficult time as the White House, Congress, The Federal Reserve, and Wall Street and even the G7 leaders were all cooperating to stave off what looked like the second Great Depression.

You shouldn't panic and make rash moves with your investments, but when you face the possibility of an impending financial calamity, you do need a special set of guidelines to carry your portfolio through until the economy rights itself again.

In the fall of 2008, when there were daily crisis meetings on Capitol Hill, many of the financial pundits were announcing that any recovery, if it were to happen at all, would take at least two years. Some were even suggesting if no action were taken immediately, the economy of the United States would grind to a halt, and that of course would adversely affect every single citizen.

When you hear this level of fear at the very highest level of our government, you must evaluate your own personal situation for the ability to weather a protracted economic storm. I want to emphasize that you are not just riding out another predictable economic cycle. You are taking steps to protect yourself so you can survive a category five storm.

In periods of economic uncertainty having a significant cash reserve is prudent. Where you may normally be comfortable with a three month cash reserve, at times like these it is important to have perhaps as much as six months of reserves. In the event that you are one of the unfortunate people who find themselves jobless as companies cut back, you need to be able to support yourself until another position can be found. I have suggested you do this previously in the chapter on savings. But in times of crisis it's even more important to employ strict financial discipline. Of course, I am assuming you would already have cut your spending down to the bone and eliminated your credit card debt and consumer loans. If you have been building our diversified asset allocation model, then you will have some of your fixed income investments maturing within a year. With a larger cash reserve and the maturing fixed income you should have the cash to survive the cycle.

If, however, you need to reduce your outlays of cash even more, one action you can take to increase the amount of cash on hand is to *temporarily* reduce your 401(K) contributions. This comes with the caveat that as soon as the economy rights itself, you should revert to your customary contribution schedule to the extent that you at least qualify for the matching funds from your employer. This action should only be used as a last resort. It is during downturns in the economy, when the markets are irrational and panicked, when we should continue to dollar cost average into our long term investment programs. It is always best to add money into an investment program when prices are down. A 401(K) plan is one of the perfect mechanisms for disciplined savings on a dollar cost averaging basis.

Another step is to decrease the extras on your payroll deductions. While it would be foolhardy not to continue with items such as disability insurance (which guarantees your income should you become unable to work), there are probably other items that are expendable if you need to bring in more cash flow starting now.

The third thing you should do now (and always) is to reduce your income tax withholding if you usually get a tax refund when you file. Otherwise you are just giving Uncle Sam an interest-free loan. While overpaying your tax bill might seem like a great way to force yourself to save, you simply cannot afford to use this tactic during a financial crisis when you are being very careful to maximize your cash resources as much as possible.

The next vital steps you should take involve strategies to protect your portfolio. In order to make sure your investment program is totally secure, it's important to be certain that you have paid off any 401(K) loans, otherwise you may find yourself with taxes and penalties assessed against your nest egg should you lose your job and there is a forced repayment of the loan. As I have said before, divest yourself of any extra concentration of stock in your employer's company. In normal times I advocate a diversification of your portfolio among ten stock holdings. In the event of a major economic crisis I would consider reducing your holdings with your employer to a level well below ten percent. This way if your company goes under, you won't lose a substantial percentage of your equities portfolio along with your job.

I would also go out of my way to secure my job if cuts seem inevitable. This is not the time to be shy about tooting your own horn and letting your employer know how valuable you are to the firm. You can also demonstrate your commitment by working extra hours and volunteering for increased duties. But by far the most important thing you can do to keep yourself from becoming expendable is to find a way to save your employer money and/or bring in extra revenue. This is also the time to step up your networking both inside and outside the company.

 During times as dire as the ones I am describing, some people even fear a run on the banks. Even though the average American did not see long lines of customers withdrawing money from their checking and savings accounts, according to Jim Cramer of CNBC it was happening on a daily basis during September of 2008. Big investors were withdrawing their money secretly on such a scale that it led Cramer to call for a raise in FDIC insurance to $2.5 million per account. Most everyone is aware of the FDIC insurance that protects each individual's bank account up to $100,000 and joint accounts up to $200,000. However, almost nobody knows that some retirement accounts are covered up to $250,000. As rescue plans evolved, these safety nets grew to a temporary level of $250,000 per account through the end of 2009.

Investment banks and brokerage houses have also come under pressure. Unlike commercial banks which use your deposits to lend to other customers, brokerages segregate your assets from theirs. This means that if you own 2,000 shares of DuPont and your brokerage collapses, your 2,000 shares should still be there and will most likely be transferred to another broker on your behalf. The accounts you hold at brokerage houses are protected up to $500,000 for stocks, bonds and mutual funds by the Securities Investment Protection Corporation. If you are holding cash in a brokerage account, you are insured up to $100,000 by the same entity. However, the SIPC limits its safety net to SEC registered investments. This means foreign currency, precious metals, and commodity futures contracts won't be covered. Naturally this protection also does not apply to losses due to poor investment choices. Most major brokerage firms will also carry additional coverage on accounts on top of the SIPC coverage for those people with larger balances. Contact your investment custodian to determine what their specific coverage is.

Fortunately you can be assured that both your 401(k) and your basic pension plan are protected from your employer by a law enacted in 1962. This law created the Pension Benefit Guarantee Corporation which has the full backing of the federal government. You should know that both your Roth and your regular IRAs are protected as well.

Even though there are many federal guarantees built into the nation's financial system, you should also protect yourself by utilizing insurance more productively. If your spouse has either a cheaper or better health insurance plan, consider switching to their plan as a dependent if you can. You may also be able to save money each month by raising your deductible. And just in case you lose the job that is providing you with your health insurance, find out what it will cost to be insured by COBRA for the maximum term of eighteen months. You should then build that amount of health insurance premiums into your cash reserves. If COBRA is too expensive or runs out, the next step is to apply to one of the short term health insurers whose contracts generally run from six months to one year. These contracts are always nonrenewable, and you run the risk of developing a pre-existing condition which may limit your ability to obtain health insurance at a later date.

The other essential is life insurance. If it is provided by your employer, you should find out if it is portable. Most likely it is not, so you would probably be better off purchasing low cost term insurance. A good financial representative can guide you as to the appropriate amount of coverage that you should have. Remember though that it would be prudent to check the cost of that insurance coverage with one of the online companies that gives quotes on term insurance. Companies such as selectquote. com and reliaquote.com are two places you could check. If your life insurance company should go out of business, you need not worry. In the past regulators have moved policies of failed insurers to healthy ones.

In the event your insurance company goes belly up, you still have protection. If you have an outstanding claim when your insurer fails, a state guaranty fund will cover it. The rules vary, but funds typically pay up to $300,000 in claims on most policies. In nearly all states there are no caps on disability claims.

For most other types of insurance you will have thirty days to find new coverage. And if you have paid in advance for something like a year's worth of homeowner's insurance, you can apply for a refund from your state insurance fund.

However, it is entirely possible that your insurance policies are more valuable than your state's limit. You would be smart to investigate the health of your policyholder and change insurers before yours defaults. You can easily monitor a company's health by checking the website of rating agency A. M. Best. This company posts press releases whenever they move an insurance carrier's credit rating up or down based on the company's financial health.

So far we have been discussing ways to protect yourself and your money. But it is equally important to look at the other side of the equation. This means finding new ways to generate income if we want to build up a reserve in case of emergency. In this dire scenario we are talking about, these are some rather drastic steps to be considered. The easiest way is to start at home. Most families can find a veritable pile of unused items that can be put up for sale.

Don't even bother with holding a garage sale because shoppers are notorious for wanting something for almost nothing. On the other hand, by selling large items to local buyers you will save the costs and hassles associated with packaging and mailing your goods. I don't know about you, but I have not figured out how to economically package a lawn mower! While holding a garage sale is free, so is putting your items on Craig's List. I am recommending Craig's List over eBay because with eBay you will incur extra charges. On the other hand, eBay affords more protection to both buyers and sellers by rating their history of satisfactory transactions.

If you don't really need more than one car, consider selling the extra one. If the market is so depressed that the price you would get would make the transaction untenable, then park your car and take the plates off so you can at least save on the maintenance costs and insurance. Just be sure to turn on your motor for a while every month to keep your automobile in working order for the day when the economy returns to normal.

Also think about using your home itself as a source of income. If you have a spare room, clean it out and get rid of any personal mementos so that it becomes rentable. If you have a small boutique hotel in your city, take a look at both the rooms and the prices there. You can then undercut the price and rent your room at the most competitive rate.

If you are not too far from an airport, you will find that members of airline crews are often interested in comfortable, affordable accommodation. You can post your space on three different websites: airlinecomuter.com, crashpads.com, and craigslist.org. Or if you are near a university, you can post your spare room on the bulletin board on campus.

The other thing you can do to utilize empty space is to consider renting it out to someone who needs a home office. There are many mothers who need a quiet place to run their business who can't do so with their children underfoot. The key is that you will have to be able to provide a designated phone line and Internet access.

Your garage may also provide an extra source of income. You may well have neighbors who have more cars than they have garage space. In some areas this kind of parking arrangement can bring in an extra $10 a day. If you live near a beach, a "park and ride" facility, or any attraction that has limited parking availability, you can charge about $5 a day for use of your driveway.

Your driveway can also generate income as a storage space for boats that are kept on a trailer. Keep in mind that marina parking lots start at a hundred dollars a month for storage space, and boat slips start at about $500. The best way to attract customers is to put your listing in the local grocery story or your neighborhood weekly.

Lots of investors have bought condos in desirable locations as second homes or for their retirement. These have increasingly become the source of mortgage defaults so most people try to rent them out to cover costs until the crisis passes. The problem is that the condo market is depressed right along with the housing market so the rents you can get are way below fair market value and may not be enough to allow you to keep your apartment. However, if you live in a city that has one or more corporate headquarters, you do have an option. Companies are accustomed to paying high rates for corporate housing either for their executives in transition or for their corporate clients to use while in town. If you happen to live in a city like New York, Washington, Atlanta, Silicon Valley, San Diego, or Miami, so much the better. These cities usually have at least one relocation service that is employed by corporations to help high level employees moving into the area. The major component of that help is finding suitable housing. Make sure your condo meets their standards and is on their list. Since leases rarely run longer than a year, you will probably be able to retake possession of your property once your finances are back on track.

As you can see, all these suggestions for earning extra money do not involve your taking on an extra job. Basically this is passive income, and that is the very best kind. But before you attempt any of the suggestions above, make sure you have clearance from your insurance carrier and that you are not violating any local zoning laws. If it is an ongoing situation, you should insist on a contract signed by both parties.

What I have described here are a host of measures to be taken during extremely precarious financial periods. The economy always bounces back eventually. All you have to do is find creative ways to ride out the storm.

Most importantly, if you find ways to cut your current expenses and increase your income, these steps will certainly serve to help you build a greater bulwark against a systemic financial crisis, whether it comes now or sometime in the future. Even better, saving, investing, and increasing your investment cash flow will always make good sense for every American, no matter what the state of the nation's financial health.

RESEARCH TOOLS FOR INVESTING

The theme of this book is how to take charge of your investments, and you can't even begin to do this if you don't know where to look for the type of information that is critical to making decisions about your portfolio. Certainly professional money managers can afford to subscribe to a large number or research resources, but there is still plenty of data available out there for the average investor and most of it is free! All you need is a computer and a few hours a week. I believe strongly that you should always try to stay on top of any financial news that impacts the equities and other financial instruments in which you invest.

I assume that you already have some money in your portfolio so my initial suggestion is low tech, to say the least: *OPEN ALL YOUR FINANCIAL MAIL.*

I know that corporate reports probably come to you on a regular basis, and it is tempting to toss them into the garbage without trying to read them. But these financial statements are an important source of information regarding a company's profits or losses, assets and liabilities, and sources of funds used to operate its business. All of them should contain a balance sheet which gives you an overall picture of a company's assets, liabilities, and equity at the end of an accounting period (i.e. quarterly or year end).

The income statement and the statement of retained earnings tell you how much revenue, expense and profit the firm has generated over a specific period of time (e.g. its fiscal year). Together these statements provide you with all the financial data you need to perform the simple analysis of finding out if the company meets my investment screens or to perform your own ratio analysis to determine if you want to buy, sell, or hold onto a stock.

I'll explain how to utilize this information in the following chapter. While much of this data is also on the Internet, there is safety in knowing that corporate reports and any other information you might receive directly from the company are accurate because they must comply with SEC regulations. However, this information quickly becomes dated because financial transactions occur continuously. Be sure you are looking at the most recent statement and continue to review the updated information on the stocks you decide to hold. Of course the best way to stay completely current is to use your computer to review the many websites that offer free information.

If you do not already own a stock, you can call or write to a company's Investor Relations Department and ask them to send you a free copy of their annual report. Reading the annual report is a great way to familiarize yourself with a company. Keep in mind though that companies try to put their best foot forward in their reports to shareholders which means the commentary portion of the report is likely to cast the company's position in the best possible light.

You can also find useful information by going to a company's web site. Simply run a search on the company name, go to the firm's home page, and look for the "Investor Relations" section. These websites vary widely in terms of ease of use and content but most will include:

- The most recent annual and quarterly reports (you may see the quarterly report referred to as the "10-Q")

- Recent news releases and access to a news release archive

- A calendar of events including planned shareholder meetings

- Notes and commentary from recent analyst meetings, speeches or other presentations.

When turning to my computer for the most comprehensive research, my first choice is usually Google Finance (finance.google. com/finance). This website gives the most comprehensive tools to find stock quotes, corporate descriptions, recent news, press releases along with the associated stock charts, upcoming events, a list of companies in the same sector, and a bevy of financial metrics. In short, if your time is limited, Google Finance gives you most of the information you need to help build and then monitor your portfolio.

My second choice is Bloomberg.com. It has a useful assortment of data that other sites including Google Finance don't offer. Bloomberg provides more information about dividends and one year performance metrics. Bloomberg charts also offer more tools for technical analysis such as Bollinger bands and MACD which are helpful for sophisticated investors. Also, if you are looking for additional news about a corporation, Bloomberg is an option which bears scrutiny.

If you go to Big Charts (bigcharts.marketwatch.com), you will find the simplest charting interface plus a vast selection of advanced charting tools if you want to use those as well. If you do venture into the "advanced charts" section, you will find even more technical indicators than those provided by Bloomberg.

Reuters.com/finance is the place to go for extensive corporate profiles and a wide variety of commonly used ratios to measure corporate performance. If you click on Reuters' "Company Profiles", you will discover the firm's cash flow per share, yield percentage, the dividend amount, the dividend payout ratio, price/earnings ratio, price/sales ratio, and the quick ratio. This resource is also valuable because if your company is considering an acquisition, Reuters will post that information and guide you to more data about the target being considered.

A visit to hoovers.com will provide some limited information for free but this website often tries to steer you into buying their comprehensive corporate profiles. Believe it or not, some of their free data is actually one or two years out of date. Obviously the is a site I wouldn't use without corroborating its information elsewhere.

If you want to find one of the most user friendly sites, you should try Yahoo Finance (finance.yahoo.com). Aside from being easily accessible, Yahoo has most of the metrics you will need. In addition to the usual corporate profile, there are links to quotes, historical prices, charts, technical analysis, news and information headlines, key statistics, SEC filings and financial information including the balance sheet, the cash flow statement, and the income statement. Another plus that Yahoo provides for free is a range of analysts' opinions and estimates for which most other sites charge.

Any publicly traded company's Securities and Exchange filings can be found on freeedgar.com. As the name suggests, this is a free site, but you can also upgrade to the subscription service EDGAR Online or EDGAR Online Pro.

Most people think of Barron's only as a print publication, but you can also go to Barron's online at barrons.ar.wilink.com for certain free annual and quarterly reports on stocks. If you are interested instead in mutual funds, visit barrons.fundinfo.wilink.com. The published version is more than just stock tables. Every week it is full of interviews, opinions, research, and articles on the markets (stock, bond, commodity, and foreign), the economy, technology, mutual funds, and interesting companies. For the dividend investor, the Market Lab section contains a table listing the week's dividend payouts. There is also a regular column of interest called Speaking of Dividends.

For alternative views of a company's prospects and current situation, you can turn to one of several stock rating publications:

- The Value Line Investment Survey provides financial information and key ratios on approximately 1,700 stocks as well as rating their "safety" on a scale of 1 to 5.

- Standard and Poor's Stock Reports give commentary and buy/hold/sell recommendations based on its rankings of over 5000 publicly traded companies listed on the New York, American, Nasdaq, and regional stock exchanges.

- Morningstar is usually the first place investors go to evaluate mutual funds. However it now produces Stock Analyst Reports on about 3000 stocks.

There is certainly a great deal of potentially confusing terminology used in the investment world. Investopedia (Investopedia.com/terms) acts like a dictionary with an extensive glossary that covers most every word you might come across.

Bankrate.com is the most commonly recommended site for anyone wanting to maximize the fixed income portion of their portfolio through CDs. In addition to a thorough analysis of interest rate trends, Bankrate.com also provides a number of helpful calculators. Surprisingly this website does not list money market rates so I must steer you to *Money* magazine for the best place to shop for that information. In addition, *Money* lists short term bond funds, CDs, and most usefully, a list of credit cards with the lowest rates and fees.

Speaking of bonds, my first choice would be to go to Bonds Online (bondsonline/information). This resource covers municipal, government, and corporate bonds, offering extensive descriptions as well as quotes. If you are interested in government bonds only, you can learn about them and buy them online at savingsbonds. gov. And, if you have decided to invest specifically in TIPS, go to the Treasury Department of Public Debt web site at publicdebt. treas.gov.

I am a firm believer in the value of REITS, and you can learn even more about them by visiting the website of the National Association of REITS' website, reit.com. For a list of all publicly traded REITS, your best choice is reitsdirectory.com.

Because I want to encourage you to look for companies that yield safe and growing high dividends, I suggest you take a look at dividendinvestor.com. The site's dividend capture calendar helps you time your purchases of dividend producing stocks.

Even though I have suggested the use of the Internet to help you with your investing, I would like to issue a couple of warnings. The first is to avoid financial chat rooms because you may encounter people who are trying to promote certain stocks for their own purposes or you may be given false information by other participants.

I would also be skeptical of Motley Fool or fool.com. They have given some stock recommendations that have turned out very badly for those who heeded them. Almost as troublesome is the fact that Motley Fool requires you to provide them with your email address. If you do, you will find yourself bombarded with solicitations to purchase their reports as they send you tantalizing emails that offer you just enough information to make you open your wallet and pay for a full subscription.

This chapter covers many sources of financial research. Some will be extremely helpful to some investors and others may not address your areas of interest. I would suggest visiting the websites that apply to you and your investment plan and then place them among the bookmarks on your computer so you can access them easily.

When it is easy to get to the information you need to buy, maintain, and sell all of the components that make up your portfolio, you are much more likely to do the homework you need to do. By staying on top of your investments you are much more likely to make prudent buy and sell decisions and prosper as a direct result of your efforts.

HOW TO READ FINANCIAL STATEMENTS

The question on every investor's mind is how to pick great stocks. Even if you get a tip from the financial media or from a suggestion from your broker, this certainly does not guarantee that you are choosing a winner.

The best way to choose a winning stock is by analyzing a company's financial statements. You don't need to be an accountant or a financial analyst to improve your chances of picking a winner. A basic understanding of the fundamentals should help you make good decisions about the various components of your portfolio.

I am assuming you have read the previous chapter and have the basic corporate information you need at hand. Now all you have to do is learn how to interpret it. I am just going to concentrate on the essentials: the balance sheet, the income statement, and the statement of retained earnings.

In order to better understand the balance sheet, you will need to follow along by looking at Exhibit 1 (along with the other two exhibits) at the end of this chapter. There you will see that the balance sheet details what the company owns, or its assets, and what it owes, or its liabilities. It also shows what the owners of the firm have themselves invested equity.

When a company is formed, the initial investors fund it by investing cash in exchange for stock issued by the company. This money is used for such things as acquiring property, buildings, equipment, inventory, permits, and supplies to fund product research and development and to hire employees. Any of this original investment that is left over is retained as cash or current assets to fund the company's operations.

If you look at the asset portion of exhibit 1, you will see that it is divided into four parts:

1. Current assets are items that can easily be turned into cash. These include bank deposits and accounts receivable. Because a company may sometimes be unable to collect all of its accounts receivable, there is usually a provision for overdue accounts.

2. Corporate investments can also be converted into cash but they carry some degree of market risk associated with their sale. A good example of this would be a portfolio of easily tradable stocks and bonds.

3. Fixed assets are permanent assets such as a factory, plant or equipment that are used to produce the product or services the company offers. These items usually have a very long life. The value of the real estate is carried at the

purchase price and therefore normally underestimates its real current value.

4. Accumulated depreciation is an accounting adjustment for the gradual depletion of long life fixed assets that allows a company to build reserves to replace them.

The other portion of the balance statement is, of course, liabilities. A company may need to borrow additional money to fund operations, buy equipment, hire extra employees or to expand. These borrowed funds are divided into current liabilities, those that need to be paid back within a year, and long term debt. Current liabilities include the following:

1. Accounts payable are debts that are usually due within thirty days. An example of this would be money owed to the company's suppliers.

2. Taxes due include payroll taxes which are owed to the state and federal governments for employees' wages. They also include the taxes due on the company's profits. These taxes must usually be paid within thirty days as well.

Long term debt is exactly what it sounds like. It can usually be paid back over a much longer period of time. Two examples of this are loans to buy additional equipment or possibly a mortgage against property. The sum of all the debt is calculated as total liabilities.

Next we move on to the equity portion of the balance sheet. It is listed as follows:

1. Shareholder equity is what I just talked about. It is the initial investment in the company by the shareholders in exchange for shares at a stated par value.

2. Additional paid-in capital is the money raised from the sale of additional shares after the start-up phase. These are secondary shares that the company hopes to sell at higher prices to the public at some time in the future.

3. Retained earnings are the profits left over that are not paid out in dividends.

The combination of these equity entries comprises the total investment held by the owners of the company. Therefore, assets, liabilities, and equity are what make up the balance sheet of a company.

However, if you are going to invest, you will also need to know how to read a company's income statement. It is a summary of its revenues and expenses and shows the level of profit or loss the company has earned over the period covered. This will make more sense if you refer to Exhibit 2 in this chapter. "Sales" is the first item you will see on the statement and gives you all the revenues generated from the sale of products or services. If it is a product, then you will see the cost of the raw materials that go into that product as well as the cost of converting those raw materials into a finished product. These items are listed under cost of goods sold.

The difference between the revenue generated and the cost of the goods sold is entered as gross profit. If you are considering a company, you probably want to see a number of at least sixty percent or higher. Usually the higher that percentage is, the better.

The category of administrative expenses encompasses all employee related costs to sell, manage, and market the company's products or services as well as any costs for the plant or equipment. When you deduct these expenses from the gross profit, you get the operating income. If the company also has additional income from interest or dividends, it is first added to the operating income before the company deducts such items as interest expense, depreciation, and taxes. The final result will be net income. Since one of the important metrics is earnings per share, you need to know that it is calculated by dividing the net income by the total number of all shares.

The third item you need to learn to read and understand is a company's statement of retained earnings. For this turn to Exhibit 3. The statement of retained earnings indicates the amount of the company's earnings, which is the amount of net income from the current income statement, added to the previous retained earnings from the balance sheet. When a company earns a profit, it must decide to do one of two things:

1. Pay out all or part of the earnings to shareholders as dividends

2. Keep the earnings to finance the purchase of additional assets, get rid of debt, or grow the other resources of the company.

If you look at the retained earnings on the balance sheet, you will see that they are the sum of all undistributed earnings of a company that it has accumulated over time. The statement of retained earnings indicates the amount of retained earnings that have accumulated at the beginning of the year plus the net income for the period you are evaluating. If management decides to declare a cash dividend, it is then deducted from the retained earnings to arrive at the balance of retained earnings for the end of the year. This is then carried forward on the balance sheet.

There are several essential things that can be learned by going over a company's balance sheet, income statement, and statement of retained earnings. There is another financial metric that I look at, and that is free cash flow. I have not included it here because it is a complex figure to arrive at, and this book is not intended to be a primer on accounting. However, you should pay attention to the items described below.

1. The balance sheet will help you find stocks that pay secure dividends. It will show you a company's ability to pay outstanding liabilities either from the liquid assets it has on hand or from the cash flow being generated from

operations. Remember to locate that cash flow you must also go to the income statement.

2. The income statement will tell you if the company is moving in the right direction and how fast it is growing. In order to make this assessment you need to look at year-over-year sales and profits. Using this statement you will be able to ascertain how much sales, cash flow, earnings, and dividends the company is generating per share. You can then use this information to analyze other important ratios. Many of these ratios are already available online as described in the chapter on research tools.

3. The statement of retained earnings is used to show you how much net income the company will retain or pay out in dividends for the year. Remember that you are looking for stocks that are capable of paying rising dividends each and every year.

You now have the basics for deciding whether or not you wish to invest in, hold, or sell a company. If you marry this information to your research tools, you should be in a good position to make qualified decisions.

There is only one problem with all the tools I have given you. There is an underlying assumption that the stock market acts rationally. In fact, the reverse is often true; the market is often ruled partly by emotion, particularly during periodic bubbles and times of crisis. Although you can no longer be lulled into buying an investment and simply riding it out for the next twenty years, you should at least take advantage of investor constants such as compounding and dollar cost averaging over long timelines as well as looking for defensive plays with high dividend yields.

The worst thing you can do is put your money under the mattress or stick your head in the sand even though there will be volatile times when merely looking at your financial statements may be quite unsettling. It is crucially important to keep a cool head, and if you can't do that, then find a good financial advisor who can do it for you. If he or she can help you sleep through the night, it will be well worth the cost.

EXHIBIT #1

Sample Consolidated Balance Sheet

For the Year Ending December 31, 2008

	December 31, 2008
ASSETS	
Current Assets	
Cash and equivalents	$12,000.00
Accounts Receivable, less Allowance for uncollected accounts (2008-$50,000, 2007-$25,000)	$30,000.00
Inventory	$191,000.00
Total Current Assets	$233,000.00
Investments, Property, Plant, Equipment	
Land	$25,000.00
Building	$175.000.00
Machinery & Equipment	$250,000.00
Total Fixed Assets	$450,000.00
Less Accumulated Depreciation	$175,000.00
Net Fixed Assets	$275,000.00
TOTAL ASSETS	$508,000

LIABILITIES	
Current Liabilities	
Current Maturing Long Term Debt	$22,000
Accounts Payable and Accrued Liabilities	$55,000
Taxes Due	$2,000
Total Current Liabilities (Short Term Debt)	$79,000
Long Term Debt	$109,500
TOTAL LIABILITIES	$188,500
Shareholder Equity	
Common Stock ($1.00 par value; 1,000,000 shares authorized; shares outstanding: 750,000 in 2008 & 750,000 in 2007	$25,000
Additional Paid-In Capital	$275,000
Retained Earnings	$19,500
Total Shareholder Equity	$319,500
TOTAL LIABILITIES AND NET WORTH	$508,000

EXHIBIT #2

Sample Income Statement

For the Year Ending December 31, 2008

	December 31, 2008
Sales	$100,000
Cost of goods sold	$30,000
Gross Profit	$70,000
Selling and Administration Expenses	$50,000
Operating Income (Profit)	$20,000
Other Income	$5,000
Income Before Interest, Depreciation & Taxes	$25,000
Interest Expense	$1,500
Depreciation	$4,500
Taxes	$8,000
Net Income	$11,000
Earnings Per Share	$10.13

EXHIBIT #3

Sample Statement of Retained Earnings
For the Year Ending December 31, 2008

	December 31, 2008
Retained Earnings Beginning of Year	$12,500
Net Income	$11,000
Less Cash Dividends	$4,000
Balance of Retained Earnings End of Year	$19,500

PROJECTED ANNUAL BUDGET

Expenses	Monthly	Annually
Mortgage on Primary Residence		
Mortgage on Secondary Residence		
Condominium Fees		
Automobile Payments		
Automobile Expenses (gas, repairs, license plates, parking)		
Other Transportation (trains, buses, taxis)		
Utilities (water, electric, natural gas, garbage)		
Life Insurance		
Health Insurance		
Disability Insurance		
Automobile Insurance		
Homeowners or Renters Insurance		
Other Insurance		
Property Tax		
Other State and Local Tax		
Food (paper products, cleaning supplies, liquor, cigarettes)		

Clothing for Whole Family		
Uncovered Medical Expenses (doctor's and dentist bills, prescription and nonprescription drugs)		
Children's Expenses (day care, babysitting, school fees, extracurricular activities, allowances, toys, school lunches, and school supplies)		
Telephone (land line, cell, and Internet)		
Cable Television or Satellite		
Household repairs		
Household Help and Cleaning		
Entertainment (movies, health club dues, dining out, sporting events, cultural events, CDs, DVDs, and video games)		
Travel		
Gifts		
Contributions to Charities or Church		
Subscriptions to Magazines and Newspapers		
Lawn Care		
Swimming Pool Care		
Boats and Recreational Vehicles		
Dry Cleaning		
Hair and Nail Salons		
Club Memberships		
Pet Care		

Accounting Fees		
Legal Fees		
Bank Fees		
Alimony and Child Support		
Income and Unemployment Tax (if not withheld automatically)		
Savings		
Savings for College		
Miscellaneous		
Totals		

Projected Annual Budget_____

LIST OF ASSETS

Real Estate Free of Mortgages		
Bank and Credit Union Inventory		
	A. Savings Accounts	
	B. Checking Accounts	
	C. Money Market Accounts	
	D. Certificates of Deposit	
Individual Stocks		
Mutual Funds		
Individual Bonds		
Bond Funds		
Limited Partnerships		
IRAs (Regular)		
IRAs (Roth)		
401(k)s		
Other Retirement Accounts		
Annuities		
Paid Up Life Insurance Policies		
Other Assets		

DISCLAIMERS

While I have the distinct pleasure to currently be employed at Crowell Weedon & Co., this book is my own work. No one at Crowell Weedon & Co. has had anything to do with the opinions expressed in this book, and in no way should anything in this book be construed as endorsement by Crowell Weedon & Co. or any of its Partners.

Furthermore the opinions are those of the author, me. As such, they are opinions and not to be relied on by anyone as the sole guidance in their investments. The information in this book is based on material and information the author had available to him at the time of publication. While the information has been cross checked wherever possible and believed to be accurate, no guarantee can be given as to its accuracy. For that very reason this book does not rely on a vast amount of statistics or quote historical rates of returns or anything else that may get in the way of common sense investing.

Furthermore each individual investor must decide for themselves what investment program is suitable for him or her. Each person must evaluate the varied risks of my programs and determine what risks they are comfortable assuming. There are risks with every investment. Some of the more common risks are Inflation, Taxation, Interest Rates, Non-Diversification, Political, Currency, Execution, Liquidity, and many others. All of these need to be considered when creating your own investment program.

Any mention of the utilization of mutual funds as an investment choice dictate that you should obtain a prospectus for any mutual fund you consider. It should be read completely with attention paid to the risks and expenses of that mutual fund. Remember that past performance is no guarantee of future results in any mutual fund or investment for that matter.

Thank you for giving these disclaimers careful consideration. It is important that you are aware of these disclosures. While we believe in the things we say, each person must assess their own individual needs and their ability to take risk in relationship to their financial resources. Therefore it is imperative that the contents of this book be considered as opinions of the author and be taken in consideration with each investor's situation. We guarantee nothing but believe in our approach as a sane, practical methodology.

www.ingramcontent.com/pod-product-compliance
Lightning Source LLC
Chambersburg PA
CBHW051513170526
45165CB00002B/457